Duct Tape Marketing

The World's Most Practical
Small Business Marketing Guide

John Jantsch

THOMAS NELSON
Since 1798

NASHVILLE   DALLAS   MEXICO CITY   RIO DE JANEIRO   BEIJING

For Carol—love always

© 2006 by John Jantsch

Published in Nashville, Tennessee, by Thomas Nelson. Thomas Nelson is a registered trademark of Thomas Nelson, Inc.

Thomas Nelson, Inc. titles may be purchased in bulk for educational, business, fund-raising, or sales promotional use. For information, please e-mail SpecialMarkets@ThomasNelson.com.

Library of Congress Cataloging-in-Publication Data

Jantsch, John.
  Duct tape marketing : the world's most practical small business marketing guide / John Jantsch.
    p. cm.
  Includes bibliographical references.
  ISBN: 978-0-7852-2100-5 (hardcover)
  ISBN: 978-1-5955-5131-3 (trade paper)
  ISBN: 978-1-5955-5146-7 (special edition)
      1. Marketing—Management—Handbooks, manuals, etc. 2. Small business—Marketing—Handbooks, manuals, etc. 3. Advertising media planning—Handbooks, manuals, etc. I. Title. II. Title: Small business marketing guide.

HF5415.13.J366 2007

658.8—dc22

                          2006031078

Printed in the United States of America

09 10 11 12 13 RRD 12 11 10 9 8

Acknowledgments

I'd like to acknowledge the following for their contributions to this book:

My parents, for allowing me to believe in everything
My brothers and sisters, for continuing to keep me honest
Mr. Heiman, for teaching me how to really read
My clients, for providing my real world education
Steve Hanselman, for being the best darn agent in the world
Michael Gerber, for pushing me to dream bigger
My girls—Jenna, Sara, Ellen, and Mary—for laughing *with* me, not *at* me
And, my wife, Carol, for your amazing example of grace.

Contents

Part I:
The Duct Tape Foundation—The Way to Sticky Marketing
(Help Them Know, Like, and Trust You More!)

Part II:
The Duct Tape Lead Generation Machine—
Turning Stickiness into a System That Works for You
(Help Them *Contact and Refer* You More!)

Contents

Part III:
Getting on a Roll!
(Find Out What Works and Do More of It)

Foreword

On the Subject of Marketing Integrity

by Michael E. Gerber, author of *The E-Myth*

I have known John Jantsch for over ten years, first in his role as a certified E-Myth Consultant for my company, E-Myth Worldwide, a role in which he served his clients and my company with the enthusiasm of a disciple, and then later as the founder and CEO of his own marketing consulting firm, Jantsch Communications. During those years, John and I would talk about business, about life, and about his personal process for growing both his business and his knowledge about business so that he could fulfill the single most important objective John has always had—to serve his clients, his community, and his family as best as any man can.

What is remarkable about John is that, unlike many men and women in this tricky world called business who claim to know the unknowable all for the purpose of enhancing their personal brand, he has remained true to who he is—a guy from the middle of America who knows himself as few of us do, and who aspires to nothing more than being a good householder and a good gentleman. But none of this modesty can hide the fact that he has spent a huge amount of the hours of his life drilling down into the practical world of marketing to discover what actually works—and why. Nor does it keep us from seeing his unique ability to teach anyone how to put this practical knowledge to work to create a wonderfully effective business.

In short, this book is really about *integrity*—John's integrity, and that of the true art of marketing—which is why I have called this foreword "On the Subject of Marketing Integrity." John and I share a passion for the subject of integrity in marketing. Marketing—which could sometimes be called selling, which could further be called getting someone hot to buy—yes, that's essentially what everyone who buys this book is looking for, even you, dear reader! After all, to everyone in business, getting someone hot to buy is obviously the holy grail. And that's what every marketing book worth its salt better be about if it's going to hold anyone's attention.

Yes, John keeps his promise, step by step by step, to demonstrate to you how to do marketing to get *your* someone hot to buy *your* something, but also—and this is very, very important—how to do it with integrity. This begs the question I'm actually raising here: what does integrity have to do with marketing? Well, first of all, without integrity, marketing is left to tricks, sophistry, and lies—the same devices the old trickster used with the peas and the shells on the streets of many cities: Is it here? Is it there? Where is it? Is it anywhere? With John, you'll not only know where the pea is, but long before you wonder, John will have told you forty-two times.

John wants to make sure you don't get lost here. He wants you to know the science of his craft, not to overwhelm you with his wizardry. In short, it's true to John's integrity that he is less interested in you thinking he is a marketing genius—there are more than enough of those out there!—than he is in delivering to you what he's promised.

This book is just like its namesake—Duct Tape—it's good, incredibly smart, amazingly practical, and immensely *sticky* stuff. You can begin to put it to use immediately.

And John tells you how. This book is also amazingly thorough. John spares no effort to dig deep down into the mechanics of marketing, as opposed to the academic clap-trap of marketing. He is less interested in the philosophy than he is in the tools, tasks, and skills required to look at marketing as a vocational school of marketing might. When you finish this book, John will want to know that you have applied it to achieve very specific results and will want you to tell him so! Yes, finally, when all is said and done, John wants to talk to you about what you've done and how he's helped you on your path. Like the good friend John is, he'll get back to you from the middle of America and ask you how you're doing, how it's going, and what's up.

I hope this has helped, dear reader. And give John my very best when you see him. He's about to become one of your best friends, too. Which is what I meant with the subject of marketing integrity. Who wouldn't want his customer to become one of his very best friends? I know I would. Wouldn't you?

A Solution to THE Small Business Problem

Why Is Small Business Marketing So Hard?

There is a reason you are reading this book. You, like countless other small business owners, want to understand how to end your marketing struggle.

Each one of you thinks your plight is unique. "Please, somebody tell me, why is it so hard to market *my* business?" In working with thousands of small business owners, this is the single question I hear most often, and the answer to this near-universal plea is the reason for this book.

You don't have to look far to understand why this question plagues so many. It really has to do with *why* folks get into starting a business in the first place. The typical small business in America is started by someone who knows how to do something. It might be how to prepare taxes, how to assemble a certain type of gizmo, how to wire a ceiling fan, how to administer a network, or how to plan a wedding. Hardly ever does this know-how include being able to market a business that does those things.

And that's the basic issue. For most small business owners, marketing is viewed at best as a nice add-on, or at worst as some kind of foreign science whose secrets are locked away in an ivory tower somewhere. Small business marketers blurt out, "I'm just no good at marketing" almost as readily as a high school student might claim he is no good at math or Latin.

But what if I told you, no matter what your business claims to do or provide, you're actually in the marketing business. That's right—*every business is actually a marketing business.* Think about it for a moment. Do you really have a business without being able to reach and motivate a customer?

The failure to grasp this fundamental notion is at the heart of the alarming rate of failure experienced by so many small businesses. If you already own a business, you may have already begun to sense this is true. If you are thinking of starting a business, I beg you to finish this book and learn everything you can about marketing before you jump into the frying pan. You simply can't afford to be "no good" at marketing if you plan to stick around and grow your business.

> If you get nothing else from this book, get this: you are in the marketing business! Marketing is an all-encompassing outlook that must inform every activity of your business.

If you get nothing else from this book, get this: you are in the marketing business! Marketing is an all-encompassing outlook that must inform every activity of your business. It isn't just a department within your business. When you discover this outlook, marketing your business gets really, really easy.

What Exactly Is Marketing?

Part of the confusion that surrounds the whole notion of marketing for the small business is the utter confusion that exists in defining marketing in MBA programs, seminars, resources, and books that claim to teach the subject.

A prime example of this confusion is found in one of the prominent marketing textbooks, *The Columbia Electronic Encyclopedia*:

> *Marketing, in economics, that part of the process of production and exchange that is concerned with the flow of goods and services from producer to consumer. In popular usage it is defined as the distribution and sale of goods, distribution being understood in a broader sense than the technical economic one.*

Now, that was helpful, wasn't it?

Kind of makes you want to fire up that old distribution-and-sale-of-goods-and-services machine doesn't it? Don't worry, that's the last textbook bit of marketing you will encounter here.

Small business marketers need a totally different definition of marketing—one that's more honest, relevant, and more like real life. Within the world of the small business, the lines between the job and life, customer and business, existence and passion are often thin and blurry. Why accept a definition of marketing that makes things even blurrier? The fact is your marketing approach is the one thing that can clarify everything and help you see your business in an entirely new way. It can infuse every decision that you make and return the passion and excitement to your enterprise.

With that in mind, try this basic small business marketing definition on for size:

> *Marketing is getting people who have a specific need or problem to know, like, and trust you.*

It's that simple.

Brilliant, you say, but if that were really the case, why wouldn't everyone just do that? One of the main reasons most businesses fail to take this approach is that they are thrown off track by the most widely practiced form of marketing: Copycat Marketing.

Introducing Copycat Marketing—Perhaps You've Already Met!

Since, as we've seen, most small business owners don't think of themselves as marketers and are too busy doing and creating, when they do turn to marketing, it is in a piecemeal, ad hoc fashion that involves basically copying what they see and hear is working for others. Trying to fill this obvious marketing void, they look around for examples of marketing from others in their industry. In other words, they practice what I like to call Copycat Marketing. In most cases they don't even realize they are doing it; they just go with marketing practices that are already the accepted norm in their industry.

Don't believe me? I challenge you to pick up any business phone directory you like, flip open to any category, and see if you can differentiate one business from another. In some cases, the ads are so similar that the owners of the business wouldn't be able pick their own ad from a group if the phone number and name was removed!

But that's how everyone in our industry does it, right? "We need a trifold brochure, business directory ad, and a Web site that begs visitors to click on our 'About Us' page." I mean, we wouldn't want to be different. What if people noticed? What if people thought we were weird?

Copycat Marketing is chock full of problems, but primarily it is a problem because it is dishonest. Think of the analogy of a gifted painter who has the ability to forge lesser works of art. All a forgery of a really bad painting produces is another really bad painting! Copying someone else's less than effective marketing is a recipe for failure.

The fact that the majority of people don't respond to most of the marketing that small businesses put out there makes Copycat Marketing a surefire way to guarantee that your marketing will fail. Your prospects don't know, like, or trust you yet, so you better give them a way to tell how you are different. Copycat Marketing simply reinforces that you are the same as everyone else they haven't heard of.

> Ostrich Marketing is practiced by business owners who simply have no idea what to do with marketing, so they do nothing—they stick their head in the sand and hope. I think you know the results of this practice.

I'm not saying that business owners who fall into this trap are being bad people. I'm just saying that Copycat Marketing doesn't allow them to tell the real story about the wonderful value they have to offer—and that's a shame! It's sickening to see businesses that can and should have a positive impact on the world dying practically unnoticed on a daily basis due to this form of marketing. Marketing should be all about putting your genius on display!

Note: It's worth pointing out that I have also encountered another type of small business marketing I call Ostrich Marketing. Ostrich Marketing is practiced by business owners who simply have no idea what to do with marketing, so they do nothing—they stick their head in the sand and hope. I think you know the results of this practice. If this is you, get your head out of the sand and jump on board now; you'll enjoy the ride!

Introduction

The Duct Tape Marketing Alternative—
How Sticky Is Your Marketing?

Somewhere along the way in my twenty-plus years as a small business marketing teacher and coach, I struck upon the ideal metaphor for my own approach to marketing practice. Just as any handyman will tell you that a roll of Duct Tape is the single most useful tool in their toolbox—one they would never be without—so I began to understand that small business marketing must be simple, affordable, always-at-the-ready, and effective at solving any of a host of problems. Yes, the trusty old roll of Duct Tape became a powerful symbol of versatility and effectiveness that flies in the face of a lot of what passes for marketing today. Every small business owner I have ever coached has embraced the metaphor as a powerful way of seeing their own marketing system.

Everyone knows, likes, and trusts Duct Tape—because it works! But let me emphasize one of the most important things about this Duct Tape notion. Duct Tape isn't an effective tool because of its color or packaging. Duct Tape is loved by all *because it sticks*. Your marketing can stick just like Duct Tape too. It can stick in the words of your staff, the minds of your prospects, and the hearts of your customers. In fact, in this book you will discover that much like Duct Tape, the more layers you apply, the more your marketing sticks!

So, simply put, *Duct Tape Marketing is a turn-key system for small business marketing—marketing that sticks, every time!*

In this book you will learn how to apply your newfound definition of marketing to your small business, and you will learn the power of applying the Duct Tape Marketing *System* to that very definition.

The small business owner who uses the Duct Tape Marketing System comes to define marketing as getting people who have a specific need or problem to know, like, trust, *and* contact you. Getting a hot prospect to actually pick up the phone and seek you out is the dream situation for most small business owners. How many times have you made the statement, "If I can only get in front of a qualified prospect, I can almost always turn him into a client"? A fully functioning Duct Tape Marketing System is the key to turning more leads into more customers.

Ultimately, with the systematic application of Duct Tape Marketing, the definition of the term *marketing* evolves to include this all-encompassing view: getting people who have a specific need or problem to know, like, trust, do business with, *and* refer you to others who have this same need or problem.

That's the value of a proven system: it delivers the keys to success every time. And it helps you leverage *more* success.

Duct Tape Marketing asks you to make that fundamental shift I alluded to earlier. It requires that you come to terms with what your business really is—a marketing business. When you truly become a Duct Tape marketer, you begin to view everything that goes on in your business—every contact with your prospect, every team member, every piece of mail you receive— with the eyes and ears of a marketing pro. And in systematizing these activities you will discover how great marketing can continuously increase each of these five keys: *know, like, trust, contact,* and *refer.*

The Duct Tape Marketing System

This book will teach you the Duct Tape Marketing System, giving you practical details on each component, including examples and exercises to help you fully grasp the key ideas and strategies. Each component was designed to fit together as a complete system, but you will also discover, as many businesses do, that the use of one component or strategy may be just enough to move your business forward.

In the first part of this book, you will learn the basics of any sound marketing, focusing on the first three aspects of *know*, *like*, and *trust* in our basic marketing definition. You will learn to identify your ideal client and then how to articulate your core marketing message. Next you will learn to develop products and services that reach these clients at every stage of their development. Then you will see how to produce marketing materials that educate your clients and attract new ones by the scores. The first section of the book will end with you learning how to get your entire team involved in the Duct Tape way. Your business will discover truly *sticky* marketing. You and your team will then be equipped to make your market *know*, *like*, and *trust* you more!

The second part of the book will build on the first three aspects of our basic marketing definition (know, like, and trust), and show you how to add the essential Duct Tape System elements of *contact* and *refer*. You will learn how to turn stickiness into a *system* that works for you. You'll do this by first learning how to run advertising that gets real results. You will then learn to enhance your media attention and expert status. You will also learn to build an education system for turning prospects into clients in the most efficient way. Finally, you will learn how to ramp up a systematic referral machine and how to automate all these *contact* and *refer* strategies with cutting-edge technology tools.

The final section of the book will show you how Duct Tape marketers really get on a roll by showing you how to *discover what is working and do more of it*. You will learn to track and manage your efforts with a Marketing Gauge. Then you'll learn the discipline of committing to your plans with a budget and calendar. Finally, you'll discover how to bring it all to life with a

Marketing Snapshot. Believe me, it's a picture that you'll want to always be in!

Remember, Duct Tape Marketing is a learning process. This book introduces some very powerful concepts and covers specific ways to use and take advantage of advertising, direct mail, referrals, public relations, strategic partnering, targeting, positioning, Internet marketing, copywriting, blogging, word of mouth, public speaking, writing, articles, coupons, promotions, lead generation, customer service, sales, and e-mail marketing.

But, more than anything else, this book is meant to be the beginning of a lifelong journey of learning, growing, and succeeding in your new marketing business. As you read through each chapter in this book, you will find that in many cases one chapter builds upon the previous one. You will also find nuggets of "I must do this today" information. I would like to suggest that you read this book with two approaches in mind: (1) jump around and find some immediately applicable tips and strategies, and (2) read it through it at least once (with a notepad and pen) with the idea of creating your entire, integrated Duct Tape Marketing System.

Part I:

The Duct Tape Foundation— The Way to Sticky Marketing

(Help Them Know, Like, and Trust You More!)

In Part I we are going to focus our attention on all of things that you must do to get your marketing business off on the right track. Completing these foundational steps is much like laying the foundation of a building. The ability of the building to stand strong in good times and bad is dependant on the strength of the foundation. These steps involve the creation of the strategies and tools needed before you ever go out there and attempt to generate a lead or a customer.

These seven chapters cover everything from identifying your ideal client to getting your entire team involved in marketing. Each chapter will help you leverage your ability to help your customers know, like, and trust you more. When you get all seven of these foundational areas working in concert, you will have the absolutely necessary foundation in place for truly sticky marketing!

Chapter One
Identify Your Ideal Client

When I talk to groups of small business owners at workshops, I will often make the statement that when you properly target your clients, you will discover that you no longer have to work with jerks. I always get a laugh when I say this, but I can also see people in the audience nod in relief.

You can choose to attract clients that value what you offer, view working with you as a partnership, and want you to succeed, but only if you have a picture of what that ideal client looks like.

> Clients who don't respect the value you bring, don't pay on time, and don't do their part will drag your marketing business down faster than any other business dynamic.

The primary purpose of this foundational step is to help you identify, describe, and focus on a narrow target of clients or segments that are perfectly suited for your business. This may actually include the discovery of several ideal segments.

I want to emphasize this notion of *ideal* for a moment. I intentionally use this term to help introduce the concept of business relationships. In healthy client/ business interactions, the idea of a relationship is at the forefront of all dealings. In a healthy relationship, both parties have responsibilities, needs, and goals. Helping each other get what they need is a given in a good relationship.

In a healthy small business marketing relationship, the same applies. So, this notion of ideal customer comes with some givens. When you create a fully functioning marketing system, one that produces predictable results, you gain the confidence to choose who you see as an ideal client. That's not about snobbery; it's about basic survival. Clients who don't respect the value you bring, don't pay on time, and don't do their part will drag your marketing business down faster than any other business dynamic.

If you don't take this step seriously, not only will it be difficult for you to grow your business predictably, you will find yourself with ill-mannered customers.

The Ideal Prospect

One of the reasons we focus so much attention on this notion of defining an ideal target client is that all clients were at one time prospects. So, in effect, what we are really doing here is getting you to define and focus on your Ideal Prospect. Much of your marketing focus, at least initially, will be on creating more and more Ideal Prospects or leads. You will eventually come to the point where you can predict with a fair amount of accuracy that if you generate a certain number of Ideal Prospects, you will in turn convert a predictable number of those prospects to customers.

Let History Guide You

One of the easiest ways to start to get this picture of who or what makes an ideal client is to take a close look at the customers your business has attracted to date. You may find that some segment of your existing business makes up a very focused market. I suggest that you create a spreadsheet of your existing customers and create as many columns as needed to add as much detail as you can about each. Start with the name of the firm or individual, their industry, the service or product they purchase, and the revenue they generated in the last three years or so. We will add more information to this, but once you complete this most basic review, a faint picture of your ideal client will begin to come into focus. Another very positive potential outcome of this initial exercise is that many business owners will then also be able to clearly identify markets that they should drop. Holdovers from past business initiatives or old directions can muddy your brand and may in fact be costing your business more than they return.

As a rule of thumb, at this point you should consider firing about 20 percent of your past customers simply on the basis that they no longer fit into the picture of your current business. That may sound a bit harsh, but I suspect that neither you nor they are profiting from the relationship at the moment. Set them up with another supplier and everybody wins.

Physical Characteristics

In order to get started drawing the clearest possible picture of your Ideal Prospect, we first focus on identifying common physical characteristics. Marketing folks call these *demographics*.

For consumers, demographic characteristics include:

- Age
- Employment status
- Gender
- Occupation
- Income
- Education level

For commercial or business clients, demographic characteristics include:

- Industry
- Number of employees
- Type of business
- Geographic scope of business
- Revenue levels

Again, this isn't a score-keeping exercise. You want to keep an eye on characteristics that your best or ideal clients have in common. Look for patterns that never occurred to you previously.

Emotional Characteristics

This is a tougher one, but may bear fruit if you can tap it. The characteristics that fall to the emotional side are what market research firms would call *psychographics*. The study of psychographic characteristics gets at the emotional makeup of prospects that may give clues to how they make decisions and whom they will ultimately *like and trust*.

Discovering common emotional characteristics is a bit more of an art than science—but it's an important art. What you are looking for here are things like values, fears, desires, and goals. What do they want out of life? What are they not getting? What do they need to know to feel comfortable? What's holding them

> Consider firing about 20 percent of your past customers simply on the basis that they no longer fit into the picture of your current business.

back? Let me stress here that there is nothing inherently manipulative in this type of reflection. The point of defining your Ideal Prospect is simply *to understand how your company can deliver the greatest value to everyone you work with.* Understanding the emotional decision-making process of your prospect is an important piece of that equation.

One of the best ways to accumulate this type of information is to retrace many of your sales calls, including the ones where you did not get the results you had hoped for. Many times, the objections, questions, and resistance that your prospects pose are really clues that you have not gained their trust or answered their emotional needs when making a purchase.

Another clue to this type of research is to understand lifestyle patterns of your Ideal Prospects. Sometimes being on the lookout for hobbies, interests, books and magazines they read, musical preferences, and travel tastes can produce a deeper glimpse into what your Ideal Prospect really cares about.

Know, like, and trust—It's a fact that people often like people who have the same interests. For the small business marketer, building business on relationships may be very much about doing business with clients who have similar beliefs and interests. This isn't a popularity contest, but all things being equal, a buying decision will tip to the business or salesperson the buyer likes the most. All things *not* being equal, a buying decision will tip to the business or salesperson the buyer likes the most—it's called human nature.

What's the Problem?

Let's revisit our definition of marketing here—*getting people, who have a specific need or problem, to know, like, and trust you.*

Without a need or problem, you don't really have a market.

So, what's the problem? What are your customers attempting to solve when they buy your products or retain your services?

I define *problem*, for our purposes, very broadly to include needs and wants. A problem may well be getting their computers to talk to each other, but it may also be a burning desire to look good to their peers.

The point is not to necessarily understand or judge what people are really buying as it is to identify and acknowledge what you are really selling. Here's the cold hard truth—no matter what you think you are selling or providing, it is the customer who ultimately determines what you are selling. You don't sell goods and services, you sell solutions to problems.

So, what do you really sell? Is it peace of mind, status, pain relief? State this revelation as bluntly as possible, and your marketing business will benefit immediately.

Location, Location, Location

For some businesses, location is a primary marketing issue. Retail businesses, for instance, commonly depend on a certain defined trading area for clients. Some businesses discover that shipping a product or even making sales calls beyond a certain area is cost prohibitive. It can be helpful to plot on a map the location of your current clients to determine if you have a trading pattern or if certain geographic areas are more desirable in terms of target market concentration.

Businesses that don't feel any real geographic constraints should complete this mapping exercise, as you may discover patterns that lead you to pockets of business. In other words, there may very well be a concentration of businesses in certain industries that you serve that you were not aware of until you actually pinpointed the physical location of each client. Hanging a customer pin map on the wall can be a fun way to keep the focus on your clients too.

How Clients Make Buying Decisions

It's important to understand how your ideal clients come to a buying decision for your product or service. Is it by committee, bid, RFP, gut feeling, referral, impulse, or some other process? Perhaps there is no real pattern here, but if you can understand a little more about how your ideal clients buy, you can focus on setting up your education system to address their decision-making process.

Best Ways to Reach Them

Some narrowly defined markets are very easy to reach; others are very difficult. One of the considerations when defining and ultimately narrowing a target market is to be confident that you can actually reach them to help them know you and learn to like and trust you and your company.

Is there an association that serves this market? Are there publications focused on this market? Can you buy mailing lists made up of this market? Can you network with this market? Add these details to your spreadsheet to help the picture to come into even better focus.

The Value Factor

One of the guiding principles of the Duct Tape Marketing approach is the ability to charge a premium for your products and services within a chosen target market.

You cannot make a market out of people who *should* need what you offer, even if they desperately *do* need what you offer. When making the final determination of whether you should narrow your focus on a given market niche, you must determine if this market values what you have to offer enough to pay a premium for your expertise and understanding of this given market.

Don't have an answer for this one? Look around for companies that already seem to be thriving in this market. You may be able to find the answers you are seeking based on some readily available information they publish (more on competitive research in the next chapter).

Is It a Viable Market?

Okay, now it's decision time. By this point you should have discovered all there is to know about your Ideal Prospect. Now you've got a decision to make. Is this a viable market?

- Is the market large enough to support your business growth goals?
- Can you easily promote your business to the decision makers in this market?
- Does this market value what you do enough to pay a premium?

Think Narrow

I want to reemphasize my call that you take all that you have learned in this chapter and commit your business to serving one or more very well-defined market niches—at the exclusion of all that don't fit your narrow ideal market description or segments.

By focusing on a very specific market niche you are free to develop products and services tailored to its specific needs. Your language and processes then can send a very clear signal that you do indeed understand those unique needs.

Many times niche markets can be easier to communicate with. A specific industry will likely have a trade association, publication, or mailing list readily available. Personalizing your marketing to this easily identifiable group and identifying them by name (construction company owners, salon owners, or chronic headache sufferers) will dramatically increase the effectiveness of your communications.

When you focus on a narrow target market, you will often encounter much less competition and hold a competitive edge over generalists who claim to also serve this market.

My Dirty Little Marketing Research Secret

I have to tell you that the one place I turn to keep myself rooted in how the world thinks and buys—you know, marketing research—is *People* magazine.

Personally, I don't really care what Mary Kate Olsen's next big move is, but for about twenty years running, more people turn to *People* than any other magazine, and that speaks volumes about what the editors at *People* have got going on. A tough thing for some small business owners to swallow is that it doesn't really matter what you like or dislike, what matters is what your target market likes or dislikes. If your target market is men and women ages 25–54, then *People* magazine is a gold mine of research for your target market. (Think it's a woman's magazine? Well, 33 percent of *People* readers are men—about 12 million.)

So, what we're talking about here is research. Read (or at least scan) *People* magazine for these reasons:

- Get a feel for what the majority of Americans want to fight, find, lose, gain, have, give, or embrace.

- See design and copy that is easy to scan, read, and digest.
- Uncover story angles that could apply to your organization's PR.

If you already read *People*, maybe you have a sense of what I'm talking about. If not, carve out an hour, go to the library, and grab about ten issues and start looking through the pages with this new view in mind. You might find some real nuggets. Plus, now you can tell your friends that you only read *People* for research purposes.

More Than One Segment

In some cases you may need to segment your market into several very distinct markets. This may be because your ideal target markets have different needs for your product, or it may be because different products or services that you offer appeal to different, distinct markets.

Many businesses practice this approach already, but when a Duct Tape marketer takes this tack, it is with the intent of creating marketing that is tailored to the needs of this specific market niche.

Don't have an ideal client yet?

To locate hot market opportunities, think about problems and ways to solve them. In other words, look for people, industries, or companies that have a problem that no one is solving and target solving them.

> The one place I turn to keep myself rooted in how the world thinks and buys—you know, marketing research—is *People* magazine.

With this approach, it doesn't really matter if they are big, little, new, or old—the defining characteristic is a need. Some of the greatest market innovations in history have taken this approach.

I read once that that Steven Jobs of Apple Computer defined the target market for the iPod as "people who didn't want to carry around 10,000 CDs." That definition likely explains why young and old, techie and non-techie could be seen snapping up iPods faster than stores could stock them.

> **Steven Jobs of Apple Computer defined the target market for the iPod as "people who didn't want to carry around 10,000 CDs."**

So what problem exists that you could solve, that could define an entire market opportunity? Is it small businesses that can't afford a certain solution? Is it people who don't need full service? Is it someone who wants something faster, smaller, or hassle-free? People who don't like paperwork? Companies that want same-day something? A market of people in transition?

Residential real estate agent Melinda Bartling decided to focus on marketing to women with changing lifestyles. She knew what she was doing had caught on when Mary, a friend she networked with, referred Melinda to a friend of hers who needed to downsize her home. Melinda thanked her for the referral and then asked why Mary didn't refer her friend to Mary's own son who sold real estate. She told her that he would have been too impatient and that she chose her because that was her specialty!

Her Web site, www.mychanginglifestyle.com, is a valuable resource for local buyers as well as sellers and women relocating to the area. Any woman coming on board with her firm also has the opportunity for meeting other women with similar interests.

What irritation in your industry does everyone just live with? When have you heard your clients or even your competitors mutter, "That's just the way it is in this business"? Start looking at things differently!

When you go searching for a target market that is hungry for a solution, there are three questions that you should also consider in order to verify whether you truly have identified a hot market:

1. *Do they want what I have?* It does not matter if they desperately need what you have. If they do not want it for one reason or another, then you are sunk. You will kill yourself trying to convince someone that they really *should* want what you have to offer. People rarely act to their own benefit unless they want to.

2. *Do they value what I do?* You must look for people who are already investing in the type, or at least the category, of service you have. Price shoppers will always be price shoppers; do-it-yourself types will always be do-it-yourself types. Look for those who appreciate the extra they get from what your solution has to offer.

3. *Are they willing to pay a premium for what I do?* This one is often overlooked and misunderstood. No matter what you sell, you don't need to compete on price.

What's on Your Refrigerator?

A big part of the ideal client profile lies in understanding what your clients value, fear, want, need, and dream about. No easy task, to say the least. It may be a bit uncomfortable going up to a client and asking, "So Bill, what keeps you up at night?" But, if you knew that, it might help you better understand how to best serve all the Bills in your market?

Here are a couple of questions that I have invented that I use with clients to help me get at this deeper level of understanding in some clever ways. Understand that this is more art than science, so you might as well have some fun with it.

I think you can tell a lot about how a person approaches life by looking into some favorite places. What do you think I could learn about you if I knew

- what is currently on your refrigerator;
- what kind of car you drive;
- your favorite books; or
- your favorite songs?

People don't seem to mind me asking these types of questions, and often the answers, combined with the demographic information I already have, complete the ideal client picture in sometimes fascinating ways.

It all means something to the marketer willing to dig deep enough to assemble the puzzle.

The Ideal Prospect Profile

Now, take what you've learned to this point and create an Ideal Prospect profile. This is simply a paragraph or two that paints a picture of your ideal client almost as though you were describing someone sitting across a table from you. Try to stay with this formula in your description: Physical description + What they want + Their problem + How they buy + Best way to communicate with them=Ideal Prospect.

Here's an example:

My Ideal Prospect is service business owner with 15–100 employees and no internal marketing department located in the Chicago metropolitan area. They have typically been in business for over 5 years. These businesses are outwardly successful and have done very little marketing. They have begun to feel constrained due to this lack of marketing.

The greatest problem my Ideal Prospect faces is that they have lost control over the various marketing initiatives and marketing materials that have been created on the fly over the years. Internally, there is no marketing accountability, and most, if not all, of the marketing responsibility falls to the owner of the business. They have also found it difficult to grow their business beyond its current market share due to increasing competition.

They desperately want to take their business to the next level.

The best way to reach these Ideal Prospects is through direct mail offering productivity tools, business workshops sponsored by trusted business professionals, and referrals from other business professionals.

This description leaves little to chance. I've even sprinkled in clues of things that this ideal client might say when talking to someone at a networking event. This type of description can help your sales team correctly identify Ideal Prospects, help referral sources refer the right leads, and help frame any advertising decisions.

With an accurate Ideal Prospect description in hand, you will eventually turn your sales calls into more of an audition. That's right—your prospects will audition to become clients. Again, there's nothing elitist about this idea; you will begin to more fully understand every action or comment made by your prospects as basic signals that this either is or is not an ideal client candidate. Many of the physical characteristics of a prospect can be determined before you ever meet, gleaned from public records and Web sites.

Once you have installed your Duct Tape Marketing lead machine, described in a later chapter, you will establish this physical description of your Ideal Prospect as the minimum requirement for accepting an appointment. Then discovering the deeper needs and emotional characteristics that ultimately make up the client relationship will become the real job of your sales efforts.

The Client Profile Tracker

While we have spent the bulk of our time in this chapter on the identification of the Ideal Prospect, I want to point out a practice that I suggest you adopt with each of your existing clients. As you read through this chapter you may have found yourself saying, "I don't know enough about my existing clients to answer that question."

So let's solve that problem from this point forward by creating the Client Profile Tracker. The Client Profile Tracker is a sheet or form that you create to keep track of as much information about your client as possible. The Client Tracker Profile will go far beyond the basic contact information of your clients and ask you to discover and record personal information about your clients such as the hobbies and interests I spoke about earlier in this chapter. Other areas may include family information and school information.

Individually this information will help you do a much better job of providing value to your clients. Collectively this information will help you understand and shift your ideal market description as well as the words and messages you use to communicate with this group. This tool can prove invaluable when a salesperson leaves your organization and a client is moved to a new salesperson.

Because of the personal nature of this information, I'm not suggesting that you send a form to your clients to complete or set up a time to interview them; just pay attention. Look around their office; listen to their stories. Ask the occasional question when a personal subject is introduced into a routine conversation.

Another added benefit of this focus on personal details is that it will make you more aware that your client is indeed a person. I know it might sound silly, but in the rush to make the presentation, take the order, and fill the goods, this fact often gets lost. This realization or focus will help you more easily make a connection and establish a relationship with your client. More than ever, I believe people want to do business with organizations that they feel they can develop a connection with—that they can *trust*.

I know that this doesn't always come easily for every business owner; use the Client Profile Tracker to help you connect.

Prospect List Building

Now that you've come this far, you should have your Ideal Prospect description or Ideal Prospect segments in hand. The next step is to go out there and find the best way to acquire a list of these prospects. This list will become your marketing gold mine.

Now, there are some practical matters I want to address here. In the chapters ahead you are going to be introduced to various ways to generate lead and clients, but first we want to establish a working group of prospects that will become the primary focus of your marketing and lead generation activity.

This prospect list will be based as tightly as possible on your ideal target description. Having said that, I realize that for many businesses this list may include tens of thousands of prospects. Do you want to market to all of them at this point? Maybe yes, maybe no. The good news is that you can decide at any point. The first step is to locate the list.

Rather than prospecting for new customers, John Jackson of Integrity Stone prefers to market his services to the tile shops, designers, fabricators, and tradespeople involved in the stone business. He developed a "hit list" of these businesses. Each month, he sends them an actual photo of a job his company has done, so they can see the kind of work he does.

For some, the ideal target market—such as IT managers at firms with 500+ employees or an individual of high net worth in a specific neighborhood—will be a small number. The point, in either case, is to find this database, purchase it or some portion of it, and start using it as the basis for your lead generation activity described in later chapters.

What do think it would mean to your marketing activity if you had just five hundred highly qualified prospects and your only job was to get them *to know, like, trust, and contact you.* Does that begin to sound like a manageable task?

That's one of the problems that small business owners suffer from. Many only need ten or twenty really good clients, but they focus attention on millions of people instead of using a laser-focused, education-based marketing program delivered to just enough ideal prospects to get the job done effectively, automatically and easily.

Database Marketing

Let me paint an intriguing picture for you. Suppose you ran an ad this week in a trade publication heavily read by your Ideal Prospect. That ad offered the readers a free report titled "The Top 10 Things You Must Know Before You Buy X" (your product of service).

As a result of that ad, twenty-seven people called a toll-free telephone number to order their free report. The names and addresses of those twenty-seven people were e-mailed to your marketing assistant who loaded them into your ACT database, assigned the introductory marketing letter task to each, and printed and mailed the letters. Each new prospect was added to your newsletter list and distributed to your sales people for a phone follow-up.

This very basic scenario is easily achievable with the use of a database marketing program. The most popular titles include ACT, GoldMine, and Maximizer. This software is often categorized as Customer Relationship Management (CRM) software, but what it really does for the small business owner is allow you to automate many of the marketing processes and successfully delegate them to others in the organization.

Web based applications such as Sunrise from 37 Signals and SalesForce.com are also enjoying widespread acceptance. There are consultants that help tailor these programs to your specific business needs.

The final action in this step is to consider purchasing and employing one of these powerful pieces of software.

Action Steps

1. Look for common characteristics such as age and gender among your best clients.
2. Uncover a common frustration among your target market.
3. Write a description of your ideal target market in terms that are easy to communicate.
4. Determine whether your ideal target market is large enough to support your business.

Chapter Two
Discover Your Core Marketing Message

Stand Out in a Crowd

Quite often small business owners will ask me to reveal the most powerful marketing strategy I have seen. I can say without hesitation that the most powerful marketing strategy has little to do with advertising, direct mail, Web sites, or referrals. No, before any of those things will really have any impact on your business, you've got to uncover and communicate a way in which your business is different from every other business that says they do what you do. You've got to find a way to stand out and stake your claim on a simple idea or position in the mind of your prospective clients.

You must discover and commit to something that allows your firm to differentiate itself in the minds of your prospects. This claim must be powerful and intentional—even if you must alter some aspect of your business to achieve it. Once this is done you must create a Core Message that allows you to quickly communicate this difference, or you will never be able to break from the grip of what I call the commodity business.

Get Out of the Commodity Business

Most prospects think that one business is essentially like the other—a commodity to be acquired by simply picking up the phone. Quite often in the mind of the market, one accountant is like another, one electrician like another, one auto repair shop like the next. It doesn't really matter if it's true or not, unless you are willing to do something about it.

The problem with residing in the commodity business is that if your prospects can't identify some specific way in which your firm is unique, they will default to the only thing they can measure—price.

Offering to simply exchange what you sell for a set price in return is one of the weakest marketing offers you can create. Price, as I suspect you've learned, is a terrible place to compete. There will always be someone willing to go out of business faster than you.

Find something that separates you from your competition; become it and speak it to everyone you meet. Quality isn't it, good service isn't it, fair pricing—not it. These are all expectations. The difference needs to be in the way you do business, the way you package your product, the way you sell your service, the fact that you send cookies to your clients, the fact that you show people how to transform their lives—it's in the experience you provide.

The Core Message Process

As you will learn in this chapter, capturing your unique difference and communicating it in a powerful manner is a multistep process.

Here's the path we are going to take:

- Discover, capture, and commit to a unique position.
- Create a Marketing Purpose Statement.
- Turn your purpose statement into a Talking Logo.
- Craft a simple Core Message to use in all of your marketing.

Ways to Capture a Difference

There are many tried and true ways that a small business can approach claiming a unique point of difference. In some cases you may already possess a unique position and simply need to identify and communicate it via a Core Message. Some businesses, however, find that they need to make a considerable shift in their business, products, services, or business model in order to create some element of their business that allows them to stand out in a way that is significant to a specific market.

> Price, as I suspect you've learned, is a terrible place to compete. There will always be someone willing to go out of business faster than you.

A home remodeling client of mine found that they had trouble competing on higher-end work. They did higher-end work, but they also did handyman type of work. They were seen as more of a construction business than the design-oriented remodeling business desired by the upper-end buyer.

When they fully understood the distinction the market was making, they changed their name to more accurately appeal to the upper-end client and started referring the fix-it type jobs to a network of referral partners.

In less than a year they completely changed the market's view of the type of work they did best, and they no longer had trouble competing for the most profitable work.

It's worth noting here that being different for difference's sake isn't enough. An identifiable target market must value the difference for it to be a candidate for your Core Message.

One of my favorite ways to create a unique difference is to

offer an Astonishing Guarantee. Can you offer a guarantee so strong that no one else in your industry would dream of doing it? The use of a guarantee as a way to reduce a potential buyer's risk has long been employed by savvy marketing people. In some circles, a guarantee has become a required aspect of the sales process.

But what if you did more? What if you created a guarantee that did far more than simply warranty satisfaction or guarantee "risk-free" shopping? What if you created a guarantee that was astonishing?

What's an astonishing guarantee? It's one that makes you nervous—and that's the point. If you could create and communicate a guarantee that nobody in your industry would even consider, you would automatically have two very powerful things going for you: a core marketing message that would *differentiate* you from your competition and a *forced focus* on delivering excellence and winning loyal, repeat customers. What else?

- An astonishing guarantee turns heads—"Try our service for ninety days, and if we don't perform exactly as promised, we will double your money back."
- An astonishing guarantee generates buzz—"They promised what?"
- An astonishing guarantee creates a mission—"Okay, troops, there's only one job—happy clients—what needs fixing?"

What could you promise that no one else would dream of? That's the start of an astonishing guarantee. Let's look at a number starting of points:

- Product—Can you offer a product that is so unique, or even trendy, that your business is associated with that offering? Or can you extend a product and offer a valuable service to make the product more useful to the customer?

- Service—Same goes for a service. Many times this can be the packaging of a service as a product. Consulting is often delivered on an hourly basis. Packaging a consulting engagement based on an outcome, with defined deliverables and fixed package price, is a very effective way to differentiate a service offering. Don't forget to give the service a powerful name!
- Market niche—Carve out an industry or two and become the most dominant player serving that industry. A really nice bonus to this approach is you can usually raise your prices dramatically when you specialize in this manner.

Susan J. Sheley of Cyndi Waldron & Associates, LLC, in Kentwood, Missouri, wanted to sell helmets, but her employer was a Harley-Davidson dealership in a state that did not have a helmet law. After noticing many riders coming in with their children, she started stocking children's helmets. When she would ask riders if they wanted to see a few of the new helmets, they would often answer, "I don't wear a helmet" or "I'm not interested."

Her reply: "Fine, but if you are going to let your child ride with you, then you better put a helmet on them because they are not old enough to make that decision for themselves."

A month or so would go by and the rider would be back in to purchase his own helmet, because the child was asking, "Where's your helmet, Daddy?" After that purchase, she would "reward" the rider with Harley-Davidson premium merchandise for the child. Susan's store effectively became their motorcycle store.

You may need to find an Internet niche search resource. One

of the ways to hunt for potential niches is find out what people are searching for on the Internet. There are some great tools for doing just that. Services that offer pay-per-click advertising also provide a great deal of keyword research "niche hunting." Many offer tools that allow you to type in a keyword, such as software training, and see how many people have searched on that and related terms in the last month.

- Offer—Can you become known by an offer you make? I know an accountant who offers his tax preparation clients a 100 percent refund on their preparation fee when they refer four new clients. They are "the 100 percent refund tax guys."

- Solve a problem—Is there something that prospects in your market fear or seem to believe is universal for what you do? If so, focus on communicating how you have the answer. Painless dentistry, for example. I know a remodeling contractor who found that what his clients appreciated the most was the way his crews cleaned up at the end of the day. He began to promote the fact that he owned more ShopVacs then any other remodeling contractor on the planet.

- Message of value—Many times there are things you do that don't get communicated, extras that you provide or services you think should be included. Your positioning might just rest in more effectively communicating what you do. I know an office furniture dealer that has adopted the message "We Make Your Business More Valuable" to communicate all the things they bring to the party. Now everything they do is focused on delivering on that statement. Everyone else in the industry sells furniture.

Steve Burbridge of Neal Harris Heating and Cooling has developed a consistent core marketing message that has successfully separated his company from the competition and positioned it with top-of-the-mind consumer awareness. The message is "Technicians You Can Trust With Your House Keys." This is used in all their marketing and even has a jingle with it for radio ads—the sound of keys jingling! How powerful is it? A stranger in a fast food restaurant saw Steve in uniform and came over and jingled his keys at him!

Below are some great ways to communicate your core message.

- Unique habit—I know a financial planner who has his clients' cars detailed right out in his parking lot when they come in for their annual review. They can't help but rave to their friends about this unique touch.
- Customer service—Everyone knows the story of over-the-top customer service provided by Nordstrom's. Create your own over-the-top customer response system, and word-of-mouth advertising will flow liberally. One of the greatest ways to kick this off is to overdeliver on your first customer contact. Give them something more than you promised, give them a gift, give them a related service for free.
- Against the competition—Many times you can create your category niche by looking for holes in the offerings of your competitors. If everyone in your industry fails to address a certain problem, boldly grab on to solving that problem and use your competition as the point of difference.
- A way of doing business—This might be payment terms, how you deliver or package your services, or how you set up your office to serve clients.

Smile Dental Spa in Tucson, Arizona, wanted give its patients a new outlook on dentistry. They pamper and relax their clients with a series of spa treatments before, during, and after their dental experience. There is some thing for everyone, even those who didn't think they liked spa treatments. Fear and anxiety are replaced with pampering and relaxation. The dental spa is disarming from the minute a patient walks through the door. The office is designed to look more like a resort than a sterile office.

- A memorable personality—This one isn't for everyone, but there are businesses that have made quite a name for themselves by adopting an odd or at least memorable behavior or character. When I was in college there was a little restaurant that was famous for the rudeness of the owner. If you were a new customer and didn't order what he wanted you to order, he would demand that you leave. The place was always packed.

Deborah Read of ErgoFit Consulting, Inc., in Seattle, Washington, took the advice of her business advisory group and embraced a character she had been using in her e-mail, ErgoGirl, an injury prevention super hero who only occasionally shows herself in public. The biggest step toward doing this was to buy a shiny red cape, which she began wearing intermittently at business networking events, including ones with Fortune 500 companies.

Your Clients Know Best

So let's dig in and create a position for your firm.

In some cases, you may have already become known for a

certain type of work or position. In those cases, your task may be to simply communicate what you already know. In most cases, however, it is not that obvious, so the best way to get at your positioning is to ask your clients. It is amazing how often your clients will be able to articulate the best positioning for your firm, even if you can't. In fact, many times I have found that business owners don't often fully understand what they do that their clients truly value.

My advice is that you ask, or hire someone to ask, your clients several telling questions. I suggest that you call up ten clients or so and ask some questions like this:

- Why did you hire us in the first place?
- What do we do that others don't?
- What's missing from our industry as a whole?
- What could we do that would thrill you?
- What do you find yourself simply putting up with in this industry?
- What would you do if you owned a business like ours?

When you do this kind of informal survey, you may hear the exact positioning that your firm already owns. Many times your clients can describe what you offer much better than you can. Asking your clients for input is a great practice no matter what you are trying to learn. Clients are more likely to refer business to you when they feel you appreciate what they think and are interested in involving them in the building of your business.

Look to the Competition for Clues

Many times you can find a unique position to claim by simply discovering gaps that no one else is filling. Study your competition as thoroughly as possible to see if you can find opportunities to stake your claim.

What You Really Sell

Another way to gain some insight into a unique positioning is to figure out what you really sell. Here's the funny thing about business. You don't sell what it is you claim to offer. You sell what the eventual buyers think they are going to get from your product.

For instance, insurance sales folks don't sell insurance; they sell peace of mind. Chiropractors don't sell neck adjustments; they sell some form of relief. In some cases businesses have little idea what they sell. If you can come to think in terms of how buyers of your products and services define what they are buying, you will be much better suited to communicate how your product or service is unique.

Capture the Core Message

Once you conduct your customer interviews, and do your competitive research and a bit of business soul searching, you must move toward refining your unique point of differentiation into a Core Message to use in all of your marketing.

You can achieve this with something I call your Marketing Purpose Statement.

Your Marketing Purpose Statement

The purpose statement is not meant to be communicated to your clients, but rather is meant to be the basis for all of your marketing and customer service activity. Think in terms of this being your rallying cry in the boardroom. This is how you want to be perceived in plain English, not polished marketing rhetoric.

A good example might be, "We're custom home remodelers, and we want to be known as the 'we-show–up-when-we-say, no-mess, no-trash, we'll-make-your-neighbors-happy, contractor.' We have hired the most professional people in the industry, and they stand out whenever we compete for business or do work for a customer. We take our ShopVac into a sales call to help demonstrate clean!"

This exercise can be fun, but it also allows you to drop the mask and really articulate the ultimate purpose of your marketing. From this you might find it easier to craft a more creative marketing message, and everyone in the firm will "get it" without the marketing polish.

Your Marketing Purpose Statement should become not just a goal but the overriding *purpose* for the business. It certainly must become a key means by which you measure your success. Are you achieving your stated purpose?

A powerful Marketing Purpose Statement should give you and your staff a vision for the future of the business.

The other very valuable use for this no-nonsense approach is that your purpose statement becomes the filter for every marketing or business decision. Does this decision, new product, ad, or whatever support the marketing purpose we are trying represent? Post your Marketing Purpose Statement on every PC in your office, and let it inspire everyone in the organization.

Have You Identified the Enemy?

One of the most powerful driving forces in human nature is competition. The desire to overcome something or some company and the need to win can in many cases be more important than the day-to-day work of the company.

One key way for your company and your people to reach a higher level of greatness and purpose is to identify and focus on beating something, on creating and communicating a reason for being that trumps your competition.

Now, understand that when I say enemy or competition, I'm not suggesting something negative. While the folks at Apple Computer will tell you that their reason for being is partially rooted in beating Microsoft, many organizations also draw motivation from rescuing things, ridding the world of things, creating peace, making life more enjoyable, teaching, sharing, spreading, and a host of other very positive things. The Apple brand stands for something positive: great design, functionality, and innovation.

And that's the point. Small business owners often have no readily identifiable group of competitors or Goliath to aim at, but they may find motivation in a great cause or reason for being, and connecting with that great cause can become the drive to play the game at the highest level.

Your cause can be grand or it can be humble, but find it and you will be much more prepared to market your business, run your business with passion, and hire people who support the cause and help improve and realize the vision for your business. Great causes possess the power of attraction.

Think what you do isn't grand enough to call it a cause?

You can rid the world of bad advertising, one ad at a time. You can prove that tax preparation can be fun. You can empower anyone to buy a home. You can make your customers so overwhelmingly thrilled they will refer their friends and neighbors willingly. You can ensure that no one will ever be afraid to go to the dentist again.

Are you starting to see how this kind of thinking and the notion of focusing on competition could help drive your actions? What if you could actually connect your beliefs and values to your reason for being? Would that provide motivation to do more? Would that start to feel like more than a job?

What is your organization's purpose for being? Aim high, and let your cause guide you, your people, and your clients to greatness.

The Talking Logo—What You Really Do for a Living

From your Marketing Purpose Statement, we move to crafting a very practical but powerful message that will eventually make up your ultimate core marketing message.

In order to really bring your Core Message to life, we will complete an exercise that answers the following question in a very powerful manner. And the question is this: what do you do for a living? The answer to that question is something that I call your Talking Logo.

When asked, most people will answer that question by telling you their title or industry. This answer offers little or no marketing value. By changing how you think about what you do for a living and turning that thinking into a marketing tool, your Talking Logo creates impact everywhere you use it.

Like a traditional printed logo, a Talking Logo is a tool that allows your firm to communicate verbally the single greatest benefit of doing business with your firm. A Talking Logo is a short statement that quickly communicates your firm's position and forces the listener to want to know more.

Remember earlier in this chapter when I asked you to think long and hard about what you really sell? Well, the answer to that question, in the eyes of your market, is what you do for a living, too.

How to create your Talking Logo? Your Talking Logo must be a short statement that leaves the listener wanting to know more. Think about your clients or potential clients . . . they want to know what's in it for them. Don't just tell them what your firm does—tell them in a way that matters to them.

"I'm in the insurance business." "I'm a painting contractor." "I'm a computer repair specialist." The only thing this type of response will get you is, "Who cares?" or worse. A Talking Logo may not really tell them what you really do, but it will force them to take note and want to know more.

Your Talking Logo is created in two distinct parts. Part 1 addresses your target market, and Part 2 zeros in on a problem, frustration, or want that market has. You know you have a great Talking Logo when a person hears you deliver it and immediately says, "Really, how do you do that?"

I have an architect client that does design/build work with large construction firms. In order to get the attention of his general contractor clients, he put the focus of his message on them. Here's his Talking Logo.

"So, Bill, what do you do for a living?"

"I show contractors how to get paid faster."

Now, if you're a contractor and you've just asked an architect that question, wouldn't you want to know more?

What about this one? "I show small service professionals how to triple what they charge."

"I help recently divorced women drastically reduce their taxes."

"I create permanent memories."

"I show young, married couples how to retire richly on what they are currently making."

"I help contractors stay out of court."

"I make weight loss easy."

"I help wealthy individuals slash their taxes."

"I teach business owners how to get famous."

Do you see a pattern?

Here's the pattern: action verb (I show, I teach, I help), target market (business owners, homeowners, teachers, divorced women, Fortune 500 companies), how to xxxx (solve a problem or meet a need).

When you read those statements above, don't you find that you want to know a little more? That type of statement alone will get you referral appointments, especially when most businesses looking for new clients simply call and ask to meet so they can sell something. Who would you see: someone who wants to sell you his work or someone who wants to show you how to make more money?

Now that you have their attention with your first answer, though, it's time to deliver the goods with a supplemental answer.

So now they utter, "Really, how do you do that?"

You must be equally prepared to answer this supplemental question. Once your prospect says, "Tell me more," you need Part 2, and that is when you tell your listener how you plan to solve his or her problem. The key to this tool, though, is waiting until you have their full attention with your Talking Logo.

Here's how Part 2 works. Again, the architect—"Well, we have developed relationships with every zoning board in the metro area and can make sure that your projects don't get hung up by red tape, making sure you get to that first pay request faster."

Again, by understanding your positioning and your target market and then communicating it through your Talking Logo, you will be miles ahead of most of your competition and well on your way to generating referrals from anyone you meet.

Step one: Create a compelling answer to "What do you do

for a living?"—one that focuses on a benefit or solution and forces them to want to know more.

Step two: Prepare a simple supplementary answer that tells them the unique way you get them that benefit or solution.

Your Core Marketing Message

Now that you have discovered the marketing purpose for your firm and answered what you do for a living, it is time to fashion the creative marketing messages you will use to communicate your purpose in a way that clearly demonstrates the benefit of doing business with your firm.

The idea, then, is to create a short statement that becomes your marketing message workhorse. Think FedEx:—"On Time Every Time or It's Free."

Laura K. Frazier owns and operates a small coffee shop in Columbus, Ohio, called Espresso Escapes. It is located right across the street from a Starbucks, so the competition is tough. She struggled to find a way to attract more regular customers. The usual stuff they tried brought some people in once, but it wasn't bringing in the repeat business they were looking for.

While driving home one day, she started thinking about what it means to be a regular at her coffee shop. As soon as she got home, she created a coupon with a very happy woman on the front that says, "Nothing feels as good as being regular!" The back of the coupon lists her location and all the reasons why it's great to be a regular at Espresso Escapes.

She left them in bathrooms all over downtown. At first, people were sort of confused by them, but they have since attracted more attention and income than any other promotion she has done.

Take a good hard look at the purpose statement and the

"What you do for a living" statement you created earlier. What is the chief benefit of doing business with your firm? What words or ideas can help you easily communicate your difference?

In the following examples, I demonstrate how a firm progresses through taking a position and then creating a Marketing Purpose Statement, Talking Logo, and Core Message.

1) My architect from earlier in this chapter realized that much of his work was design/build, a process that generally asked the contractor and architect to act as a team in the completion of a building. Contractors who brought them into projects liked what they offered the project team. The architect also noted that while contractors and developers vigorously embraced the idea of design/build, most architects only entered into this type of arrangement when required. In fact, while most of the larger construction firms advertised their design/build experience, no architectural firm did so.

The architect decided to position his firm as the design/build architects. They needed to convince contractors that they were "contractor friendly," especially since contractors controlled many of the design/build decisions.

> *Marketing Purpose Statement: We want to be the architect that shows builders the only way to work with architects in design/build contracts.*
> *Talking Logo: We help design/build contractors get to the first pay request faster.*
> *Core Message: "The Contractor's Architect."*

2) An electrical contractor heard his clients complain about the quality of work of other contractors and the lack of timeliness in completing that work. His primary clients were new homebuilders. New homebuilders hate callbacks and really hate delays that disrupt the somewhat delicate building schedule.

Marketing Purpose Statement: We want to be known as the one electrical contractor who will show up when we say we will and do the work right the first time.

Talking Logo: We help homebuilders eliminate callbacks.

Core Message: "Wired Right on Time."

3) A window cleaning business realized that many of the firms they competed with were very poorly operated, unprofessional, and not likely to be around for very long. They wanted their prospects to understand that not only was window cleaning something they were good at, it was something they were passionate about.

Marketing Purpose Statement: We want people to know that we treat window cleaning as a profession, that our people are true professionals who treat the homes they enter as they would their own.

Talking Logo: We help homeowners see a better world.

Core Message: "Your Pane Is Our Passion."

Some other examples:

- A remodeling contractor: "On Your Job Until It's Done—Forever"
- A shopping center: "You Know What You Want, We Know What You Expect"
- A financial planner/CPA: "Full Circle Financial Advice From a CPA"

How to Communicate the Difference

Once you find your chosen strategy or combination of strategies to differentiate your business, all of your advertising and promotion should be centered on shouting about that difference. Commit to it, stay at it, and resist the temptation to wander off in the next new direction. Building your unique brand takes time and patience. The payoff, however, is what differentiates the winners from the losers in this big marketing game.

Action Steps

1. Revisit your target marketing description.
2. Interview up to ten clients to focus on why they buy from you.
3. Complete the Marketing Purpose Statement.
4. Create your Talking Logo: "What you do for a living" exercise.
5. Create a core marketing message.

Chapter Three

Wake Up the Senses with an Image to Match Your Message

When it comes to your business, a properly executed identity can set the expectation for your client or potential client's experience with your firm. I don't want to overdo this notion; this is nothing like "creating the optimum brand experience" or other mumbo jumbo that you might read in a branding book. I just want to communicate that the little things are big when it comes to small business, and while you don't need to spend a fortune on an identity consultant, you should take the time to get the details of your image right.

First impressions are vital, and when it comes to making them, the eyes are the first participants. The eyes consume vast amounts of information and relay it the brain unconsciously, as Malcolm Gladwell has shown in his fascinating book, *Blink*. It's this process that allows humans to (right or wrong) make snap judgments about whether something appeals to them or not. In many cases, this snap judgment is all that your firm will ever receive.

For the small business, the visual aspects of the firm are rarely given the attention that they deserve. Intentionally choosing and defining your company's "sense of style" in a way that helps to support all of your marketing messages and introduce your firm to potential clients assures that you make the right first impression. You should invest wisely in the creation of compelling identity elements that effectively wake the senses of your ideal client and communicate that your brand means business. You only get one chance to make a first impression, and you need to take your best shot each time you get the opportunity.

The Elements of Identity

If asked, most would list a company's name and logo as the primary elements of a brand. While those are indeed important elements, Duct Tape marketers expand this to include the entire scope of elements that could come under the heading of style. Any time that a client or a potential client comes into contact with your firm, they are experiencing your firm's brand or style. If you accept that definition, then you quickly see that any list of elements must also include:

Stationery	Business cards	Attire (uniform)
Forms	Invoices	Fax cover
Telephone manner	Customer service	Advertising
Delivery vehicles	Salespeople	E-mail format
Printed materials	Signage	Web site
Office facility	Employee attitudes	Vendors
Smells	Sounds	Tastes

All of the items listed above, as well as your firm name and logo, either support your company's image or detract from it.

The Role of Your Identity Elements

The image elements of your brand perform very specific functions. Like many things related to your business, you must understand their purpose before you can determine which elements are right for your business.

Because your logo or an advertisement for your firm may be the first thing that a potential client comes into contact with, they must perform this task:

- Clearly identify your company.
- Appeal to your target market.
- Differentiate your firm.
- Support the most important aspect of your Core Message.

When defining image elements for your firm, you must ask if every element meets these criteria.

What's in a Name?

The name of your firm goes hand in hand with your logo. In some cases, such as in a phone directory listing, it may be the only element that the potential buyer experiences.

The name of your firm has several functions and should be chosen with at least one of these in mind:

- Recognition of your products or services—Is it clear what your firm does? *Bob's Electrical Repair* is stronger than *Bob's Electric.*
- Differentiation—Does your firm name allow you to stand out in your industry? In the legal field, *Smith, Jones & Williams* could be replaced by *Traffic Violation Busters.*
- Favorable association with the target market—If the clients of your exclusive salon are primarily upscale women, then *Smitty's Hair Palace* might not make sense.

What Does Your Logo Say?

The company logo is the cornerstone of your firm's branding elements. For many firms, the logo is the visual reminder of everything that the firm stands for. While a great logo won't necessarily build your firm, it plays a vital role in representing it. Conversely, a weak or confusing logo can detract from the value that your firm brings. Here are the elements of a good logo:

- It has a lasting value—Trendy logos don't hold up over time.
- It is distinct—Some amount of uniqueness, as long as it doesn't confuse, is valuable.
- Appeals to your target market—If your target market is partial to blue, then it doesn't matter that you're not.
- Supports your Core Message—If you are trying to communicate your low, low prices, then your logo should support that image.
- It is legible—This seems pretty obvious, but many people use typefaces and images that can't be printed or carried to a large sign. Your logo should clearly identify your company, and it can't do that if people don't understand it.

Can You Attach a Visual Metaphor?

While it is not always available, a logo or name that evokes a visual metaphor can be a very powerful tool. For instance, the name Duct Tape Marketing has the tendency to convey much more than the name of a company or service. The relationship to the concept of low-cost, effective marketing that works is inherent in the metaphor of Duct Tape.

In many cases, colors and powerful images can help drive an association to your business and help you stand out. Red trucks, catchy names, a vivid image, or a mascot can all help when it comes to standing out.

Jennifer Katus of ClearLaunch Consulting, LLC, in Unionville, Connecticut, needed to build awareness of her company's name and contact information among executives with her former employer so they could reach her if they needed her services. She decided to capitalize on Daylight Savings Time, so she handed out mugs and notepads with a tag labeled "Spring forward with ClearLaunch," a reminder to turn their clocks ahead the following weekend, and her Web address. It reinforced her company's name, Web address, and image as a clever planner.

Seek Professional Help

A professionally created logo is worth the investment. Having said that, there are many very reasonable designers and services that specialize in creating logos for small businesses. You may also find online services such as LogoWorks.com can provide good service at a reasonable price. When you look for a logo or graphic designer, make sure that you are able to communicate the following:

- A description of your ideal target market
- Your Core Message and any other supporting messages that you want to convey
- A list of all of the ways you might use the logo: business cards, packaging, advertisements, clothing . . .
- Lists of colors or shapes that have either positive or negative connotations in your industry

- Examples representing your competitors, or the industry as a whole

After a logo is developed, ask your designer to complete a package that contains some or all of the following:

- Stationery, including business cards, letterhead, envelopes, and thank you note card sets
- A template that can be used as the base for forms such as invoices, memos, work orders, agreements, and fax covers
- A sales presentation template. Do you have salespeople making proposals and presentations? Create a standard tool that meets with your other identity materials.

This little extra effort can produce consistency that will help your image hold up over time.

Your Identity Standards

Once you have established a look and feel for your printed materials and stationery, have your designer create a set of standards that you can publish and distribute to every person in your organization.

This set of "graphic standards" can be a simple document that describes the way in which your logo can be displayed, where logo files are stored, and the exact color usage and type styles that are to be used in ads, letters, and forms.

This basic set of standards can help slow the inevitable misuse and inconsistent use of graphic elements related to your brand. If you document these basic standards and share them with employees and vendors, your image elements will enjoy a consistent look.

Wake Up the Senses with an Image to Match Your Message

The Telephone

The way your phone is answered sends a marketing message, yet most business owners don't give it a thought. Prepare a script and set of standards for receiving calls and stick to it. This may include a short sales message or tone when answering the phone.

Give serious thought to how a receptionist takes messages or checks to see if the caller is important enough to be sent on to the boss.

Your Voice Mail

Create a script for your voice mail that reinforces a marketing message. It can be creative while getting the message across. Create one way and have everyone in the firm adhere to it. Please don't tell me that you are either on the phone or away from your desk.

How about a short message about a new product, a tip, or relevant quote?

Your E-mail

E-mail is a place where people really trip up their brand. Create an e-mail template complete with contact information and a marketing message-based signature and make sure that everyone adheres to it. This is not the place for clip art and fun wallpaper to appear.

Sights, Sounds, and Smells

Your work will generally represent the state of your working environment. Even if your clients don't visit your place of business, it should look as though they do. Set standards for your place of business (even if that's the home office) as though a new prospect was expected to show up at any minute.

Dress

Do you need a dress code? Remember, dress, like every other element in this chapter, either adds or detracts to the brand you want to portray. One of the great things about owning your own business is that you can hang out at your desk in your flip flops with your favorite old dog at your feet and nobody can tell you to do otherwise. But know that how you choose to dress does impact your market's impression of your ability to deliver the goods.

So you may not have a dress code, but your market does. I heard a speaker on this subject comment that you should dress just a little better than your market. From a small business marketing point of view, I like that advice.

Logo apparel has also become a very acceptable small business uniform of sorts.

Your Mini Billboard

The business card, while commonly accepted as a form of communication, is greatly underutilized as a form of marketing.

The basic elements of the business card must be in place: the company name, logo, address, and all contact information including e-mail and Web site.

The business card also offers the opportunity and space to promote an aspect of your marketing story or even generate leads by offering a two-step product such as a free report, workshop, or newsletter. Most people only print on one side of their business card. The back side should give them some very compelling reason to ask for more information, call, or visit your Web site.

Pamela Dawn D'Azzo of Oz Video Productions in Carrollton, Texas, always has a current calendar printed on the back side of her business cards. She finds that people are much more likely to keep the card (and keep it handy) when there is convenient information printed on the back. Everyone needs access to a calendar at some point. She provides one along with her company name and number.

Of course having this information on your business card is only half of the battle. You must also get your card into people's hands. Here are some tips for turning your business card into a low-cost marketing machine:

- Always carry them with you (you never know when you might bump into someone in a line somewhere who needs what you do).
- Hand them to anyone you meet in a business setting and ask for one in return (it makes you more memorable).
- Put them in everything you send out (invoices, letters, etc.).
- Give them to anyone who asks for your phone number or e-mail address (your child's teacher may know someone who has a need for what you do).
- When people ask for your card, give them two and ask them to pass it along to someone else who might need it.
- Look for unique ways to distribute your business card (strategic partners might let you place them at a reception desk, place them on community bulletin boards, consider the local pizza shop—a lot of pizza gets delivered in some neighborhoods).

When MaryAnn Soukup, a CPA located in Leawood, Kansas, formed her practice, she found that certain referral sources only sent one type of client her way. Although appreciative of their referrals, she needed to encourage them to refer other types of clients, too. Additionally, she wanted a marketing tool that was more substantial than a traditional business card.

She solved both problems by developing an 8.5″ x 3.5″ brochure that features a tear-off business card. One side highlights her specialized services; the other side presents her bio. It is a unique tool that gets noticed at networking functions and easily slips into an envelope for follow-up communications.

Process as a Marketing Tool

Any successful business got that way because they practiced systematic approaches to marketing, selling, manufacturing, implementing, consulting, delivering, and customer service.

When I say systematic, in this case I often mean unconsciously systematic. A business or salesperson finds a strategy or tactic that works and repeats it, at least to some degree. Really successful businesses take this a step further—they document this successful system so that it can be accurately duplicated by many other people.

When you begin to understand that your business is really a marketing business, you see these documented systems for what they really are—proof that you know what you are doing or, better still, a tool to help communicate how your firm is unique.

Every one of your marketing, fulfillment, delivery, and customer service processes or systems should become a marketing element. How about a name? Give each of your systems and processes names, and they will become valuable marketing assets.

- A sales call: Our Two-Step Internal Seminar
- Your guarantee: White Glove, We-Don't-Rest-Till-You're-Happy-System
- Your service call: Annual ROI (return on investment) Guarantee Evaluation
- Your customer service: Postsale Satisfaction Check-up

- Your delivery of a service: Ten-Point Value Implementation Process
- Your referral process: 100 Percent Refund Process
- Your customer loyalty tactic: Birthday Surprise Bash

Naming a simple system may seem like overkill in some businesses, but it forces several very positive marketing activities. When you give a system or procedure a name, these kinds of things happen:

- It's more likely that you will actually document and utilize the promised system.
- Your prospects may view the existence of such a system as proof that you do as you promise.
- Documented and named systems give your prospects a feeling of consistency and professionalism—both good things.
- By giving names to even the simplest processes, you will experience greater buy-in from your team members asked to operate the systems.
- Named systems and processes can be a very powerful way to reinforce your Core Message and brand.
- Documented and named systems and processes are a great starting point for industry articles and workshop topics.
- Documented and named systems and processes are fertile breeding grounds for new products and services.

An Identity Audit

One of the first steps to improving your image is to take a good hard look at where you stand. You accomplish this by auditing your existing materials and measuring the positive or negative impact they have.

If you are just starting a business, then this lesson will help you identify the best way to get your image off to a good start. If you already have a business, then an identity audit is the first step to strengthening your company's identity.

Much of your firm's identity or brand elements are experienced at the subconscious level. People don't sit around and analyze every detail of your marketing materials; they just know that they either like something about them or they don't.

One of the best ways to experience how much work your subconscious mind does is to enter a place of business that you have never visited and conscientiously take note of everything that you see, hear, smell, or feel. When you step back and do this, you might see just how much impact all of these factors have on your senses and consequently on your judgment of the business. This is the exact same process that your client goes through with your firm on first contact.

Now take a walk around your own business with heightened senses. What have you overlooked? Call your business, ask someone to fax you a document, visit your Web site, and mail a letter to yourself. It is imperative that you understand how much impact these seemingly little things have on the overall effectiveness of your marketing.

Do the same with your competition. Call them, write them, visit their Web site, and ask them to send you some information. Take note of how they accomplish these tasks and how they impact your impression of the firm.

It can also be helpful to gather opinions of a group of customers. I find that customers like to be asked what they think and will often offer very insightful information when given the opportunity.

Duct Tape Marketing Chapter Resources

LogoWorks - Logos and graphic design
www.ducttapemarketing.com/logoworks.php

Action Steps

1. Determine if your identity elements support your target market and Core Message.
2. Create identity elements for your marketing, sales, fulfillment, and customer service processes.
3. Complete your identity audit.
4. Consult a professional graphic designer with target market and Core Message in hand.

Chapter Four

Create Products and Services for Every Stage of Client Development

So far we have looked at marketing in terms of a target market, Core Message, and image. In this chapter, we turn inward to take a look at the products and services you offer to this target market to get their attention, permission, and business.

Visionpace, a Midwestern software development firm, offers its prospects free white papers (technical podcasts and training from nationally known experts). Many of these prospects also take advantage of their software coaching process, and eventually some of these firms engage them to create custom software.

By having several ways for prospects to access the company's products and services, Visionpace slowly builds relationships with prospects and clients as it offers them more products and services.

A Different View of Products and Services

Too often, businesses develop one core offering and hope to sell that and only that to a target market. This all-or-nothing approach is limiting from a marketing standpoint. Marketing is really much more like dating—first a movie, then dinner, perhaps dancing, and then, maybe, marriage, raising children, and spending the summers in your mountain hideaway.

Duct Tape marketers attempt to move their target prospects

along a logical path toward a group of offerings geared to address the various stages of client development. This gradual, trust-building approach allows businesses to charge much more for their products and services while enjoying a much greater relationship with their clients. And the process of marketing becomes much easier.

The Client Stages Defined

Once you define your Ideal Prospect and determine your target market characteristics, you really only have what I like to call a group of suspects. You suspect that they may need what you have to sell, but that's it. The point of your initial marketing to this group is to get them to identify themselves as a true prospect so that you can gain permission to market to them.

Eventually, through continued systematic efforts, some number of these prospects become clients and then become repeat, premium clients and, eventually, champions and a prime source of referrals. But each stage is attained by applying specific marketing strategies and offers to gain an identified action.

So let's recap the stages:

- Suspects—The list of people who fit your target description
- Prospects—The list of people who have responded to an offer for more information
- Clients—The list of people who have tried your product or service
- Repeat Clients—The list of people who have upgraded or purchased more
- Champions—The list of people who tell others and sell for you

The Marketing Funnel

You may have heard of the notion of a marketing or sales funnel. In this model you attempt to generate leads on a broad scale and then "funnel" them toward becoming a client with increased contact and content. This funnel concept is incomplete when it comes to the small business, as it leaves out the entire notion of what you might do with your clients once you get them to make a purchase.

The Marketing Funnel Turned Upside Down— The Marketing Hourglass

The greatest opportunity for real growth in most businesses comes from selling your existing clients more products and more expensive services and from the referrals generated from those clients. The marketing hourglass takes the idea of funneling suspects into your marketing machine and adds the intention of expanded product and service opportunities—thus the hourglass. This approach asks you to develop a very deliberate series of marketing, product, or service offerings with a specific intent:

- Automatically qualifying your prospects
- Gaining their permission to allow you to market to them
- Offering a low barrier or trial product/service
- Focusing on overdelivering on the purchase
- Moving the client to other opportunities or levels of service
- Generating word of mouth or referrals

Marketing Offers by Stage

The Duct Tape Marketing System involves the creation and promotion of offers that act as paid marketing tools to first turn suspects into prospects and then prospects into customers. That's right, done properly, this process actually allows you to get paid to market your services. These marketing tools, in the form of free or low-cost information and workshops, can attract the interest of prospects and help begin to build trust while intentionally moving the prospect toward a buying decision—all the while as you produce revenue to fund your marketing machine.

Marketing Offer for Suspects

Your suspect database responds to offers of complete information designed to help them solve a problem or answer a question.

These take the form of free reports, tips, white papers, workshops, demonstrations, evaluations, newsletters, books, guides, and checklists. We will look at how to attract your suspects to these offers in the next chapter, but you must begin to develop a product in the form of a free offering before you can move beyond this step. Examples of this type of offering might be free reports with these kind of titles:

- 10 Things You Must Know Before You Hire a Roofing Contractor
- Tax Slashing Secrets of the Rich Revealed
- 7 Simple Steps to Building Your Own Greenhouse
- 12 Ways to End Back Pain Now
- How to Cut Your Software Training Costs in Half

Marketing Offer for Prospects

Once your suspects raise their hands and request your free report, they are giving you permission to market to them. As prospects, you have a much better feeling that they are qualified to become clients, and you can justify moving them to the next level by offering them some more. Your prospect list is now ready for an offer to become a client.

In many cases this requires a low-cost or trial service offering to gain the ultimate trust needed to become a premium client. You may need to create an introductory product or version of your service that can be priced low enough to offer a low barrier to becoming a client. Think of this as your foot-in-the-door offering.

Your Clients Become Premium Clients

So now we enter the expanding shape of our hourglass—our marketing mix—as we move clients to deeper engagements and higher-priced products. Clients become premium clients when they respond to offers for repeat business, higher pricing, or custom services. You must develop products and services with the intention of creating premium clients. This may include membership offerings, upscale consulting engagements, or even service agreements and products and services from strategic partners.

Once your clients move to premium status, the focus is to also find specific ways to turn them into referral sources.

Premium Clients Become Champions

Some amount of your clients will automatically become champions. These are repeat clients who voluntarily look for ways to promote your business. In effect, this potent group can become your informal sales force. With this group you need to develop promotions and offerings that will help them refer business or even come to see referring business as something that is of great benefit. Memberships and affiliate programs that promote and reward loyalty will work well to motivate this group. (In chapter 11 we will cover referrals in great depth.)

So let's bring this concept together by looking at an example of what The Marketing Hourglass system might look like for, say, a consulting business:

- Suspects: Free newsletter, workshop, or teleseminar (a seminar that is conducted conference-call style)
- Prospects: $79–$149 Self-study training courses
- Clients: $500–$2500 Group training program
- Premium Client: $25,000–$40,000 Annual Engagement
- Champions: Promote group training/strategic partners

Ways to Create New Services and Products

Service to Product

One of the most effective ways to market a service offering is to turn some aspect of that service into a product. In this way, you can give a complicated, sometimes invisible service the right name, a package, and a fixed price. When you are trying to get a client to know, like, and trust your company, offering them something of value that is easily understood and communicated can give you a leg up over the other service providers who are a little fuzzy about what they are offering.

Gabor Wolf of the Marketing Commando in Budapest, Hungary, employs a unique market research process to determine with laser accuracy what products his customers want to see developed next year. He asks his customers this question: "Next year we're launching products A, B, C, and D. These products will be sold at full price next year, no exception. However, you can choose one, and only one of them, and as soon as the product is launched, you can buy it at a significant discount. Please select the product that you want to buy at a discount next year!"

They phrased the research question in a way that makes

customers think a lot harder and makes it impossible to give the wrong answer. They have found that customers consistently purchase the products they selected in their research.

Extend a Product

On the other hand, your product offering might very well receive a boost down the road if you can find a way to attach a service to the product after, or in addition to, the initial sale. Many companies have found that their real profits come from servicing a product that they practically give away.

Package Your Knowledge

Few things enhance your expert status and appeal more than information products that show or tell prospects how to do something. Again, it's proof that you know what you are doing and can allow you to build trust in very powerful ways. These information products can be used as marketing lead generators or as low-cost trial products. In some cases they can allow you to reach and serve markets that don't make sense for you or your staff to serve personally.

Joe Crisara created a promotion for his heating and cooling business called "The Oldest Furnace Contest." The promotion was such a success, $367,000 in sales, he went on to create an entire business, Big Time Business Development Services, devoted to teaching HVAC contractors how to create similar promotions.

Bundle and Package

One way to create a new offering is to bundle several products or services together and offer special bundle pricing. Subscription services that include monthly fees or annual commitments in exchange for a new package offering is one way to bundle.

Complete offerings that include products and services from

strategic partners can allow you to create a product or service with a broader appeal than you might otherwise create on your own. In some instances, you can get strategic partners to add valuable products and services in exchange for the exposure they gain by being introduced to your clients.

Offer Levels of Service

One way to extend your service offerings is to offer gold, silver, and bronze service levels that allow clients to purchase a certain level for a certain price. Some businesses find that they can offer group programs at a different level of price than individual programs. Another take on this strategy is to take larger, more complicated service offerings and break them into logical parts.

License Your Knowledge

Many successful small business owners have found that they can ultimately increase their product offerings by allowing other businesses to learn their success formulas. This is particularly effective in vertical markets. If your dry-cleaning business has cracked the code for growing repeat business, there may be a market for hundreds of other dry-cleaning businesses that want to learn your secret. The opportunities that come forth by this type of industry leadership are generally astounding and well worth the effort to develop this type of offering.

Write a Book

Matthew Kounkel of Kounkel Chiropractic in Leawood, Kansas, learned that writing his own book, *YOU 1.0*, allowed him to market through different mediums not previously available. By being a published author, he gained instant credibility and access to potential radio spots, newspaper features, speaking engagements, etc. It also functioned as a marketing tool, further cementing why a customer should do business with him. Prospects see him as an expert in his field (www.kounkelchiro.com).

Look for Holes in the Hourglass

What products or services, partnerships, entire new ways of thinking need to come to life in your business in order to have something to offer your clients at every stage of client development?

Like an ongoing theatrical performance, your business has many contacts with potential clients and clients on the way to a fully developed relationship. One of the surest ways to ensure that the play is flawless is to map every instance and manner that your business touches its prospects and clients. This process also reveals the gaps and missing products or services you should be aware of at all times. By creating this map, your firm can then decide what it needs to do in order to deliver the experience that your marketing messages promise.

Price Is a Function of Value

Almost every small business I have ever worked with doesn't charge enough for their products and services. This is due in part to a lack of confidence, part to a feeling of competition, and part because they have never strategically educated their clients as to the value of what they have to offer.

Want a raise? Raise your prices. When you take the complete marketing hourglass strategy to product and service offerings, coupled with the education approach presented previously in the marketing kit, each and every one of your offerings become more valuable as they are enhanced by the complete offering.

For the most part your premium products will only be marketed to highly qualified clients who already know, like, and trust you. They will expect to pay a premium for these premium products and if presented correctly, they will feel privileged to do so. That's not a statement of arrogance as much as a statement of what people choose to do when they are allowed to appreciate value.

Raise your prices right now, today. By the time you finish this book, you'll feel confident that you have done the best possible thing for your business.

Action Steps

1. Understand the client stages.
2. Develop marketing, product, and service offerings that address every aspect of the marketing hourglass.
3. Map every point of customer contact and look for holes in the hourglass.

Chapter Five

Produce Marketing Materials That Educate

Educate, Don't Sell

Done well, marketing can eliminate the need to sell. In fact, no one likes to be sold anything, *but they do love to buy.* Your marketing materials can do the job of selling if you focus on creating a set of materials that provide an education for readers—an education that compels them to buy.

Most small business owners can't really articulate why someone should buy from them. This is a place where Copycat Marketing is as its worst. Lacking a compelling argument, many small business owners attempt to fill brochures with nice sound bites or product descriptions. This type of marketing, typically housed in the tri-fold brochure, does little to help you stand out in a crowd, let alone educate.

In this chapter you will learn the steps used to create a tool kit of marketing materials that are flexible, affordable, personal, practical, and, most importantly, educational. The very process used to create these materials will provide you with a valuable education as well. The simple process of documenting your organization's most compelling features can, in itself, help bring clarity to the real benefits your firm has to offer.

The Marketing Kit

The Duct Tape Marketing tool of choice for marketing materials is something I call a marketing kit. The marketing kit is a collection of carefully crafted, individual pages of information that help you present the best possible case for why a prospect would buy from you. The kit format allows you to create personalized inserts, frequently changeable and updateable inserts, and inserts tailored to the specific needs of a prospect.

The term *kit* helps describe the interchangeable fashion of the documents. The documents contained in the kit are assembled as needed in a carrier, such as a pocket folder, and then produced quite often in-house on the increasingly affordable high-quality desktop printer.

There are instances where higher quality offset printing is called for, but for most small quantity needs, it is hard to beat the "on demand" nature of the marketing kit. You always benefit from presenting a professional image, but the content is the most important aspect of your educational marketing materials.

I suggest working with a graphic designer to create a custom pocket folder and then create complimentary design for a template sheet to be used when you print your individual pages in-house. This way you get the benefit of offset color printing for your base sheet. Among other things, the marketing kit contents should include your case statement, your difference summary, your ideal client/customer description, your marketing story, and your offerings.

In addition many people find very cost effective design templates from firms such as StockLayouts (www.stocklayouts.com) can do the trick. This company features agency-quality market template designs that are perfect to incorporate into your marketing kit creation.

Your Case Statement

Over the course of the last twenty years, I have had the occasion to work with several very large nonprofit agencies. One of the things that all nonprofit agencies must get good at to survive is asking for money. The standard tool used in fund-raising is something called a case statement.

A case statement, as the names implies, is a document created to make their case to the donor—their answer to why anyone should give them money.

When you think about it, there's not that much difference between the profit and nonprofit sectors. Almost every small business is proposing that the prospect trade money for something of value. I have found the case statement to be a handy tool for cutting through the marketing hype and getting to the real reasons why prospects should trade their money for what you have to offer. Your case statement should address the following:

- A statement of a challenge, frustration, or problem that your target market experiences
- An image of what life is like when the problem is solved
- How they got here in the first place
- A path for them to follow
- A directed call to action

Here's an example of a case statement for an expense auditing firm:

A Case for Waste
Money is a terrible thing to waste.

Do you know that there may be money hidden in your trash and energy bills?

For the most part your business runs very well. You attract clients and provide a product or service as promised. What you may not know is that your operation could be leaking profits from some very unexpected areas . . . your trash disposal and energy consumption. It's a fact that profit comes from one of two places—increased revenue or decreased expenses. Successful firms rely on sales and marketing to increase profits and increasingly on industry experts to slash expenses.

But do you really know everywhere to look for hidden expense charges?

What if there was a way to know for sure that you were maximizing every dollar of your trash disposal and energy consumption costs? What if there were a firm that had the specialized expertise to look for ways to lower your costs and increase your efficiencies, and what if the services of such a firm didn't cost you a dime? You would have to take a look, wouldn't you?

Maybe it seems easy enough, but our experience tells us something different.

Successful savings in the waste disposal and energy consumption business starts with an understanding of how these industries really work. There are firms out there today that might suggest that you can save money by switching your service to them. There are firms that act as brokers for large national services, but when you stop to think about it, is their motivation saving you money or getting your business?

We don't get paid until we perform.

Saving our clients money is our only motivation and the primary way we get paid. Our consulting fee arrangement is based on receiving a share of the savings we create for our clients. With that mind-set we had to develop a host of unique ways to save our clients money and help them recoup past overcharges. (A surprising percentage of our clients have been overcharged by vendors for years.) We are one of the only true waste and energy consulting firms in the country. Our consultants have years of experience in the waste and energy business and can analyze every aspect of your waste and energy expenses. We tailor our recommendations to your specific needs without any bias toward one service provider or another. Ask yourself, with this mind-set what would you have to lose by contacting us to learn more?

Waste Stream Monitoring has the expertise and the tools.

Waste Stream Monitoring has been helping firms control and reduce their waste disposal and energy consumption costs since 1995. We have developed proprietary savings strategies and a nationwide service network along with cutting edge technologies and tools. If you would like to learn more about Waste Stream Monitoring or receive a free, no obligation evaluation of your waste and energy expenses, contact _____ at 913-831-4800, or visit the Waste Stream Monitoring on the Web at www.WasteChek.com.

Your Difference Summary

Use this page to hit them with how you are different and shower them with benefits of doing business with you. Don't tell them what you do; focus on how you do it. Tell them about your unique approach, your processes, and the little things you do. If you have studied your competition and you know what your target market craves, make a point to summarize your solution. I like to keep this one to the top three or four things that you do that your target market will value.

Your Ideal Client/Customer Description

People generally feel more comfortable working with companies that specialize in their unique industry, niche, or problem. Describe your ideal client. Describe why they typically hire you—what's going on that makes them reach out to you? Describe the factors that seem to exist for your most successful engagements. Outline the results they typically enjoy when they engage your services. By completing this description you will narrow your market in number but make yourself substantially more attractive to someone who fits your ideal description.

Your Marketing Story

Many companies have interesting or even gut-wrenching histories. Tell them your story in an open, honest, and entertaining way, and you will win their hearts as well as their heads. The ability to connect by way of personal stories is one of the greatest advantages that small businesses possess over big businesses. The marketing story is an effective tool because it allows you to do several things that traditional marketing or advertising does not.

- Stories are an effective way to simplify a complicated issue.
- Stories can create emotion. People buy on emotion and rationalize their decision with facts.
- Stories are easier to remember because people can more readily relate to a story.

Most importantly . . . stories build trust. There are several very effective formats and devices for marketing stories:

- Client: Stories that demonstrate to the reader through a client story the value of doing business with your firm

- Who: Stories that allow the reader to connect with who you are or who the company is
- What: Stories that communicate what your firm does in a way that gets at why it does it
- Where: Stories that paint a picture of where your business is headed
- Values: Stories that illustrate slogans like "we try harder"
- Lessons learned: Shared lessons that expose the human side—both the good and the bad

Here's an example of a company story for a window cleaning business.

"This is a tale of passion"

I fell in love with window cleaning at an early age, but it is my mother who I credit with the success of my window cleaning business.

Faced with raising five children on her own, Mom determined that each of us would learn the necessary skills to survive in the world. I learned to cook, clean, and even sew by the time I went to elementary school. One of my favorite lessons involved sewing. Each of the children picked a material and pattern, learned to sew it together, and then, to assure we took the lesson seriously, each of us was required to wear the new outfit to school for one entire day.

Cooking around the Noon household was a rather simple and orderly affair. If stew came out of Mom's large army pot on Sunday then you knew what you were eating the rest of the week. For breakfast she would cook oatmeal, always oatmeal. Now she did possess a bit of marketing knack, for each day she would use a food coloring to present us with a different color of oatmeal.

Growing up I didn't mind the chores so much, but I was never able to master the art of dishwashing, so I did a great deal of chore trading. What I learned was that I loved to clean windows and that my brothers and sister did not. So I always washed the windows in our home, and people said we had the brightest, shiniest windows in all of town.

Now, what they didn't always know was that Mom had developed a special concoction of window and glass cleaner. Her secret formula, as I now call it, is what helped me launch Noonshine Window Cleaning Service just over ten years ago.

While we've grown to be quite a force in the glass cleaning business, that secret formula, the one that keeps our customers singing our praises, has never changed. In fact, we got so many requests for our window cleaner that we decided to bottle it up and make it available to the entire world. And that's what you are holding in your hand right now.

Noonshine Window and Glass Cleaning Formula is an environmentally friendly glass cleaning wonder that leaves windows, shower doors, mirrors, chandeliers, and other surfaces shiny. While other glass cleaners leave a film on your glass, ours never will.

So now you know why I say, "Your pane is my passion."

Bill Noon

Your Product/Service Offerings

This page should outline the various services, products, and packages that you have available. Clearly describe and detail the benefits of each.

Case Studies

Pick representative clients or industries, and outline how your product or service solved someone else's challenge. Case studies allow the reader to see themselves getting relief. An effective case study format states

- the situation
- the problem
- your solution
- the result

Case studies are even more powerful when they contain photos of your client, project, or solution accompanied by a testimonial quote from the client. Over time you can collect more and more of these and draw upon the ones that fit an industry or problem that is relevant to your prospect.

Involve Your Clients in Telling the Story

Case studies have long been recognized as an effective way to offer proof that your product or service does what you say it does. The idea behind this tool is that prospects can read how you helped someone just like them and come to the conclusion that you can repeat that performance. The only problem, though, is that most case studies I come across don't really do much—it's like people know that they should have them but they really don't know how to create them.

Here's my advice. If you want to write a really good case study, involve your client in the creation of it. My method is to actually set-up an interview with a client, with the communicated intent of getting their help in the creation of their story. (Oh, and in case you didn't jump to this conclusion yet, this is great way to resell them on being your client.) There are many ways to structure a good case study but, at the very least, I like my clients to answer these four questions:

1. What solution were you seeking when you hired us?
2. What did/do we provide that you value the most?
3. What has been the result of working with us?
4. What would you tell others who are considering hiring us?

Now package those answers up on a one-page document and move on to about ten more clients for the same. This tool may become your greatest marketing weapon in a world of prospects looking for an authentic marketing story to latch on to.

It should be no surprise that the actual users of your services are better prepared to offer great marketing copy for other prospective users, but few business marketers take advantage of this resource.

Testimonial Proof

Third, party endorsements are another way to add proof that you do indeed deliver as promised. Collect quotes from real live clients and create a page titled "See What Others Have to Say about Us." Try to get quotes that focus on the results you have helped them realize. These quotes can be some of the strongest selling tools you have. New technologies make it easy to create audio and video testimonials too. Here are some suggestions for acquiring powerful testimonials:

- Craft some proposed testimonial copy and present it to your clients for approval.
- Ask a prospect to obtain a testimonial from your clients (they will copy you).
- Photograph your clients using your product or associating with your brand.

A Simple Way to Get Great Testimonials

The best time to get a testimonial is when you are standing face to face with a client and she tells you what a great job you have done. (Learn to pounce on this moment of truth.)

Here is a simple testimonial system that works every time. Purchase a two-column business card holder and ask your happy client to give you two business cards. Ask the client to write a brief testimonial on the back of one card and then place one with the testimonial facing up and the other next to it.

Testimonial tip: when you ask clients to write a testimonial, ask them to write it as though they were recommending your business to a friend who was considering hiring you or buying from you. You will get a much more powerful tools than if they are writing it to you.

This little collection of cards will become your sales trophy case and will lend instant credibility to your claims. It is obvious that the testimonials are genuine because they are on the person's business card. This little trick also helps clients overcome procrastination because they can complete the task while you are standing in front of them. Over time you will build a very impressive showing of testimonials. (Obviously you can transfer these quotes to Web sites and other marketing materials.)

Frequently Asked Questions

Some of your prospects will come to you with very specific questions. If you can address them in a succinct manor, you may not have to do much more. Start by going over the types of questions you receive from clients, sales prospects, and even e-mails.

Sometimes this can be a good place to start all of your marketing materials. After you answer some of the most persistent questions, go back and make sure that these answers run throughout your other pages as well.

Bill Caskey of Caskey Sales Training in Indianapolis, Indiana, gave me this tip. Create two sets of FAQs. One is the basic list of questions that clients ask and the other is a list of questions you wish they would ask. He called this second page "Questions That Should Be Frequently Asked" and found that this page helped him teach his prospects things they didn't even know to ask. (www.billcaskey.com)

Client List

Make a list of clients as a way to demonstrate who else trusts you.

Processes and Checklists

With this page you should show the reader how you do what you do. Create detailed checklists and flowcharts that show your prospect how you keep your promise. In many cases, you have these anyway, but by making them part of your marketing, you can demonstrate how much more professional your organization is.

Documented process description will help justify why you charge a premium for your services. Many people underestimate how much really goes into delivering a quality product or service—so show them.

Articles

Have you written articles for publications, newsletters, or internal distribution? Include relevant reprints and press clippings.

Something for Everyone

At this point you may be wondering if everyone will really read all of this. The simple answer is no. Some will pore over it, some will skim, and some will take solace in the fact that you have it. People learn in many different ways, and the job of the marketing kit is to address as many of those ways as possible. Most prospects will need to know one or more of the following:

- How you work—process, case statement, FAQ
- Results you achieve—case studies, testimonials
- Who you know—client list, case studies
- What you know—process description, articles

Web Content That Educates

The next chapter goes into great detail about your Web site content, but I wanted to let you know at this point that most of your marketing kit content is great content for your Web site as well. Your Web site can and should have the same educational tone.

One Way to Get All of This Done

Creating a marketing kit is a fairly large and important undertaking. Don't try to do it in one day. Create an outline for each page you intend to create and then just start working away. You may also find it helpful to purchase a small digital recorder and start talking into it. Many people are better at communicating by talking than by writing. You can always get someone to interview you on tape and then hire a copywriter to turn it into well-crafted written pages.

- Create your outline.
- With outline in hand, pick a page and start writing.
- Don't edit, don't answer the phone, don't do anything but write.
- Once you complete this step, put it away and come back to it tomorrow.

- Go over your document again and rewrite and edit.
- Get someone else to edit and proofread.
- Consider getting feedback from several ideal clients.
- Move to the next page.

How to Use Your Marketing Kit

Marketing kits are not intended for mass, direct-mail campaigns. They are much more effective once you have generated a lead and want to proceed to fully educating the prospects. Many of your competitors will not possess anything as complete as your kit, so you should use it to your advantage:

- Mail it to leads prior to a sales call.
- Use it to educate your referral sources.
- Leave it behind after a sales call.
- Produce it in a downloadable format to store on your Web site.

Thinking Beyond the Basic Kit Format

Victor Gonzalez of *The Logic of Success* in Alpharetta, Georgia, created an interactive marketing kit. As a speaker, he needed to get his message out. Instead of sending out your basic video demo like everyone else, he decided to take a different approach. He collected mini-video clips, his reviews and testimonials from past speeches, his book, *The Logic of Success,* and created a simple five-page Web site. He then took the Web site and used an AutoRun CD software package to create a CD-ROM that loads on startup and simulates a Web page off-line. All the links to articles, reviews, videos, etc., are active.

Next he mailed out twelve hundred in simple sleeve envelopes. His theory: if they won't come to his Web site, he would bring his Web site to them. The total cost was $3,200. He garnered fifteen speaking engagements at an average of $2,500 plus travel per engagement. Great ROI!

Duct Tape Marketing Chapter Resources

StockLayouts - Stock graphic design layouts
www.ducttapemarketing.com/stocklayouts.php

iStockphoto - Stock photos and images
www.ducttapemarketing.com/istockphoto.php

Action Steps

1. Define the three or four key benefits that make your firm unique.
2. Collect ten testimonials from satisfied clients.
3. Develop four case studies that demonstrate results you or your products have delivered.

Chapter Six
A Web Site That
Works Day and Night

I'm not sure how it happened, but somewhere early on in the formation of the Internet somebody decided that Web sites weren't marketing tools, so the content and design didn't have to relate in any way to the rest of the marketing activity. Millions of small business owners rushed out and hired "Web designers" to work on "that part" of their business. I can't tell you how many small business Web sites I have visited that just don't make sense. I've seen Web sites that:

- Don't feature the company logo
- Have spinning doodads that do little but distract
- Are impossible to navigate
- Don't have an address or phone number—anywhere
- Have entirely different core messages than the rest of the marketing
- Don't adhere in any way, shape, or form to other marketing collateral material

In this chapter we are going to cover the basics of using a Web site to promote your business. Notice that I didn't say we are going to discuss whether or not a Web site is right for your business or not. If you don't already have a Web site, heed this warning: harness the Internet or prepare to become obsolete.

This text is not meant to be a complete discussion of everything to do with the Web; there are some great books on the subject and many qualified consultants who can help in that regard. This chapter is designed to give your business a marketing edge when it comes to using a Web site and the Internet to spread your marketing message, educate your prospects, and convert prospects to clients.

The Purpose of a Web Site

Many small business owners were originally seduced with the notion that all they had to do was put a Web site online and wait for the phone to ring. When that didn't happen, some became disillusioned and either left the Web or left their Web site to languish as little more than a place to collect dust. For a Duct Tape marketer, the primary purpose of a Web site is to act as a tool to integrate and connect all of your marketing communication and education.

If you don't already have a Web site, heed this warning: harness the Internet or prepare to become obsolete.

The good news is that the educational content outlined in the marketing kit can be the perfect base of content for your Web site. You must drop that Copycat Marketing notion that tells you that you need a home page and an "About Us" page just like everyone else. The purpose of your Web site is to allow your visitor to begin the task of more easily knowing, liking, and trusting you.

Much like your marketing kit, your Web site can educate,

persuade, and motivate your prospects to take action. But a Web site can also provide a much richer set of benefits as well.

Benefits of a Content-Driven Site

Awareness

These days you are expected to have a Web site if you are in business, and many prospects start their search for a new product or service before they ever pick up the phone. This is even true of prospects that are referred to you.

Shorten Selling Cycle

In many cases, with a rich content-driven Web site, your prospects may feel that they can trust you before they even meet you. I have dozens of clients that have found so many answers on my Web sites that they were ready to hire me the minute I showed up at their office.

Access to Your Information

A Web site offers your prospects access to your marketing materials whenever they wish. You can and should save the contents of your marketing kit online and direct your prospects to your Web site to acquire the information.

Tool to Refer Your Business

A content-driven Web site allows referral contacts to share a great deal about your firm by simply directing referral prospects to your Web site. In fact, a great strategy is to create a page specifically for this purpose. If you have a referral source that consistently refers prospects, you can even personalize a page on your site for them: "Welcome, friends of Bill Smith"

Automate Distribution of Marketing Information

As you will learn more fully in Chapter 12, a key component of the Duct Tape Marketing lead generation machine is to promote the distribution of free or low-cost information and tools that allow your prospects to get to know you. A Web site can provide a valuable interface for the automation of this process.

Capture Lead Data

When someone reads an ad on a billboard, they may make note of a service, but they may not need that service for months. By that time, your billboard is no longer in sight. One of the fundamental tools of a Duct Tape Marketing Web site is the ability to exchange premium information for the visitors' contact information. Once you capture this information, you have the key to begin marketing to this prospect for months and years, assuring that your ad is top of mind when it's buying time.

Your Marketing Kit as Content

Much of the content outlined in the marketing kit should also appear on your Web site. In many cases you may need to shorten some of the content as it is harder to read long blocks of copy on a computer screen.

> Use the case statement as the home page content. Don't waste this page with some sort of a "Welcome to our Web site" message.

I like to use the case statement as the home page content. Don't waste this page with some sort of a "Welcome to our Web site" message. Hit your visitor with the most compelling marketing copy you have. After that, you can have some major components:

- Your difference
- How you work
- Your story
- Your ideal client
- Your products/services
- Case studies
- Client lists

As a rule, I like to sprinkle testimonials throughout a Web site. Even better, get an actual photo of your client to go with their testimonial or case study. There are a growing number of simple tools that also allow you to add audio testimonials to your Web site. Imagine the power of a client's testimonial in his voice.

Search Is a Verb

Much of the power of Web sites as a marketing tool is being driven by the enormous growth in the use of search engines as a way to find products, services, and professionals. Even prospects that simply want to find a new auto repair shop in their town are turning to local search tools to locate local businesses.

While you may not have any dream of ruling the search engines, your business can benefit locally and nationally by adhering to a set of simple content, design, and search engine factors outlined below.

Seek Professional Help

There is no question that Web design, programming, and search engine technologies can be confusing. You may never have the desire to learn how to write HTML code or anything to do with how your Web site works. But your Web site is one of your most powerful marketing weapons, and you must be very involved in how it supports your business.

There are many, many very qualified Web designers and search engine experts. In most cases, your business will be better served if you seek out a professional to delegate this task. You cannot, however, abdicate this task simply because it seems too technical. If you do, you will wind up with an expensive Web site that does little or no good.

Learn as much as you can about the workings outlined in this chapter, and then go to a qualified designer with some very specific instructions. Make sure that you are fully prepared to discuss your ideal target client, competitors, Core Message, identity elements, and any Web sites that you like when you first visit with a prospective designer.

A Word about Design

Simple. That's it. Keep your Web site design simple. You can create or hire someone to create a very professional Web site that is focused on getting your content found and read. Many designers have a tendency to overdesign. You need to balance the need to look good with the need for search engines to find your site and visitors to consume your content. Don't present them with distractions.

Simple also applies to images. Search engines can't see images and only view them by a couple of very simple attributes. Images can add visual interest, but keep them simple and lightweight.

On the technical side, look for a designer that is very fluent in CSS (Cascading Style Sheets) design. I don't have the space to go into the full technical nature of this, but a designer using CSS for Web site design will be able to produce a site that more effectively takes advantage of the power of search engines.

Page Layout

Start each page with a powerful headline. <u>Follow each headline with a highlighted introductory paragraph</u>. Your intent is to grab readers and quickly guide them into the rest of the page.

Simple Navigation

At one time it was common practice to create images for navigation bars. Again, these images don't help in search terms and can bloat the loading of the site. Ask your designer to use CSS techniques to create text-based but visually interesting navigation links.

Make sure that a six-year-old could navigate your site. In fact, that may be a good way to test it. Create links to every page and add text links within pages from one page to another to give the user lots of ways to jump from point to point.

Shoot Your Web Designer if They ...

Suggest flash intro pages. These are pages that do all this really cool animated motion graphics and then present you with an entry or splash screen. Flash intro pages may be visual works of art, but unless your visitor came to your site to be entertained, they don't really add any value and can't be read by search engines.

Suggest frame pages. These are sites that often present right-side navigation in one frame and then main content in another. Again, this type of site design hurts your ability to be found by search engines.

Suggest templates. Web site templates can have some appeal as they are generally very inexpensive, but often they are heavy on images and don't allow you to match your Web site look and feel to your other identity elements.

Expert Content Sites

Holly Russo of Wavian Web Design in Gaithersburg, Maryland, has another seemingly unrelated way to draw customers to her Web design business. She maintains a page about parakeets, a hobby of hers, on her business Web site. Although unintended as a marketing draw, she receives over five thousand visitors a month to her extensive FAQ page. Sometimes other bird lovers contact her through this page and end up hiring her for Web design.

Because of this, she often advises her clients to create informational pages of all kinds that help draw traffic to their Web site. Even topics unrelated to business can be used as a tool to gather traffic (www.wavian.com).

Blogs and Additional Sources of Content

Another way to enhance your Web site content is to take advantage of add-on technologies and resources.

Blogs

A blog is a diary-style Web page that has become very popular with business Web sites in the last few years. Blog software allows you to update and add content very easily. This can help you build a relationship with a loyal audience and give them a reason to come back to your site.

The often personal or specific nature of most blog content also makes them a great tool to extend and demonstrate your expertise on a topic of interest to your prospects. Most blog software allows you to very easily create and add content to a section of your Web site.

The best business use of a blog is to create a tightly themed topic blog for some important aspect of your industry or specialty and post deep amounts of information that will attract search engine interest and develop a following that cares about the content.

Dave Seitter, a construction attorney with a large Midwestern law firm, used a blog as the center of a construction-related portal called MidwestConstructionLaw.com. He found that the blog allowed him to easily post topical, even fast changing, information and draw search engine traffic far beyond that of a traditional static Web site. The site was crucial in positioning him personally as an industry expert.

Resource Center

Create and display content and links to other industry resources. Think about other types of products and services that your target market is interested in and provide lots of information on other Web sites.

Article Directories

There are any number of online article directories that allow you to search for topic-specific articles and reprint them on your Web site. This can be a great way to add depth to your content and give the search engines more reasons to find you.

Syndicated Content Feeds

Many publishers allow Web site owners to easily syndicate ever-changing content via RSS feeds. This technique allows you to publish up-to-the-minute news headlines, for instance, that impact your target market. Good content, ever-changing, keyword specific—all good things.

Creative Commons Content

A Creative Commons license is a tool that allows creators of content to place conditions on their copyright. Many allow you to make use of their content through this system. This includes images and content. Yahoo even has a Creative Commons Search Directory.

Basic Search Engine Optimization (SEO) Tips

You may never actually get involved in the programming aspects of your Web site, but I think it is important for you to be aware of these basic terms and tips so that you can communicate their importance to your Web designer or programmer.

In fact, make a checklist of each of the elements below and question your designer's intention to utilize each in your Web site's design. You know you have a very good fit when you find a Web design firm that asks you about these elements up front.

Keywords

No matter what your business does, you must understand as fully as possible what terms your target market uses to find products and services like yours. There are databases that track the actual number of times certain search terms are used by surfers.

From these databases it is important that your Web page content, titles, and headlines contain the most important search terms. Search on the Internet for keyword database tools and you will find many varieties.

A good use of the idea of keywords is to think in terms of giving each of your Web pages a keyword phrase theme and then making sure that the theme phrase appears in a number of the elements introduced below.

Title Tags

Title tags are part of the HTML structure of every Web page. Think of them as the informal name of the page. Search engines use the content in a page's title tag as one of the primary ways to categorize what the page is about. It's an important page element, but many people waste or misuse it.

Use title tags or page names that are descriptive and search friendly. Instead of "Welcome to Bob's Used Cars" for a home page title tag, use "The Greater Muskogee Area's Best Deals for Used Cars Are at Bob's." The reason this is a better title tag comes down to how people search for Web sites. Unless they know the name of your business and search specifically for it, your company name as a page title isn't very useful.

Links to Your Site

Search engines will give your Web site higher marks if they see that other Web sites in your related industry also find it worthy of linking to. Your site will benefit from trading links with like-minded businesses.

Don't get caught up in the link farm, trading with pages and sites that only want links in quantity. Focus on sites that you think would add value for your visitor. Only contact sites for link exchanging if you are certain that the site owner provides high-quality content that is relevant to your business and your target market.

When I find a site that meets these qualifications, I try to write a very personal note to ask to exchange links. There are software programs out there that automatically look for linking partners and even send out generic linking invitation e-mails. To have any success with link swapping, you need to be very personal. Link to the site in question first. In your note include your reasons for linking, and state something you really appreciate about the link prospect's site.

Anchor Text Hyperlinks

Many Web sites have links to other pages on their site such as "Home" or "About Us." I guess that these links get the job done, but they don't really tell the search engines about your site. Use descriptive text and search phrases for links. Use "Great Used Car Deal" as a link to your Bob's Used Cars site or "Find a Construction Attorney" for your link to your roster of construction related attorneys

Use Heading Tags

HTML, the Web's programming language, uses a series of *H* or *heading tags* to help structure a page like an outline: H1 for the most important headings, H2 for subheads, and so on. Each of your pages will do well to contain a keyword rich headline, much like an ad for the page, and H1,/H1 markup in the code to let the search engines know that this is a really important part of the page. Then, do the same with subsections with H2,/H2 tags. I know that most designers understand these tags when it comes to styling a page, but few get the important role they play in the search engine game.

Create Site Maps

A site map is a page that has links to every page on your site in a structured manner. Visitors may not often find much use for this page, but search engines may use this page to find and index all of your site's pages.

Each of the major search engines has developed ways to submit and update your site map. If you work with a Web designer, make sure that you inquire about each of the above tips. Take this book with you to meet with your Web design firm and demand that they either address each of the elements in this chapter or explain why they don't think it is important. The world of Web sites and search engines is a fluid, ever-changing world. You must constantly pay attention to the changing landscape or at least make sure that you are comfortable that your chosen Web designer is on top of the latest trends in Web design and search strategies.

Local Search Is Here to Stay

A rapidly growing number of people are using search engines to find local businesses much like people traditionally used the phone books. Every major search engine has rushed into this local search market and have created directories and search platforms focused on delivering local search results. If you want the best pizza in Cutbank, Montana, you search for "best pizza, Cutbank, MT," and the search engines will deliver up three area pizza joints with phone numbers and maps.

If you have any desire to do business locally, you need to make sure that each of the major local search engines—Google, Yahoo, MSN, AOL, and Ask.com—has your business listed. Each engine has a unique process for registering. In addition to registering with local directories, there are a few things that you can do on your Web site to add local flair. Remember, someone searching for a remodeling contractor in Austin will enter "kitchen remodel, Austin, TX."

Local Title Tags

This is probably one of the most important bits of information on your page, so make sure your title reads something like "YOURFIRMNAME Kansas City's oldest bakery."

Local H1 Tags

Make sure that your keywords for your site and your geography have H1 tags—"The Best Baked Brioche in Peoria, Illinois," is an example of a local-based headline that you would enclose in H1 markup.

Content

Add your local address and phone number early and prominently to every page, and don't forget to list the suburbs you serve. Look for ways to add local content of value. For businesses such as insurance, real estate, financial planning, and other professionals looking for prospects in local communities, lists of community events, senior activities, school districts, and church functions may be a great way to extend your business content into the communities you serve.

Local Internal Links

Make your internal links local friendly—instead of "Accounting Clients" use "Omaha Accounting Clients."

Schloegel Design Remodel, a residential remodeling firm located in Kansas City, Missouri, found that when they featured their project portfolios with city-based link text they started to rank highly in the search engines for these geographically based searches. They used terms such as *Kansas City kitchens* and *Kansas City baths* for link text instead simply using something like *our kitchens* or *our baths*.

Local External Links

Another strategy for local-oriented businesses is to identify area businesses that may serve your target market or that your target market might find useful in some manner and build a local resource section on your Web site. After you build your mini local directory, invite businesses that you included to link back to your site. Don't forget to include the name, Web site address, brief description of the site, and the city and state in your listings. These elements combine for some very nice local content.

Duct Tape Marketing Chapter Resources

Yahoo! Small Business - Small business Web hosting
www.ducttapemarketing.com/yahoo.php

Action Steps

1. Rework your marketing kit content for your Web site.
2. Find a Web designer that understands search engine optimization.
3. Locate sources for additional Web site content.

Chapter Seven

Get Your Entire Team Involved in Marketing

Okay, we've come to a pretty significant juncture in the process of laying the foundation for truly sticky marketing. If you've completed a number of the key exercises and suggestions so far, you've begun to collect a set of very powerful marketing assets. These assets will allow you to venture out into your market and confidently declare, "Come and get it!"

The next section of this book is dedicated to the act of lead generation or getting your prospects to contact you. This is all about turning your stickiness into a system that works for growing your business. But before we move to this next all-important step, it's vitally important for you to take the foundation you've built in these last few chapters and share it with your team—even if that team is only one other person.

This chapter suggests several ways to infuse your entire staff with a firm understanding of the core components of your new marketing business and to excite them, perhaps for the first time, about playing a role in the launch and growth of your marketing business.

Marketing Is Everyone's Job

If you accept that your business is essentially a marketing business, it's not much of leap to grasp that marketing is, to some degree, everyone's job.

Most of the time, small business owners completely disregard the idea of what might be called "marketing training." But then they wonder why no one in the organization gets pumped up about providing over-the-top service. Or why no one really has a clear picture of who and what makes an ideal client. What if everyone if your company was made to understand that part of their job, no matter what else they did, was marketing? Can you imagine an organization with a culture like that?

Here's the scary part. Everyone in your organization that comes into contact with your clients or prospects is performing a marketing function. The question is whether they are performing it with a marketing intention or not.

Conference Calls Unlimited, a telecommunications firm in Fairfield, Iowa, did something that set them apart from their competitors, not only in the conferencing industry, but also in most retail operations. They focused a great deal of their marketing education efforts on inspiring their employees and contractors. By focusing on employees, they ensured those employees would be inspired and enthusiastic with each interaction with a customer. They worked on making the workday day fun, productive, and inspiring.

They streamlined everyone's responsibilities to focus on priorities: 1) making the customers happy, 2) making the prospects happy, and 3) making each other happy. The goal for the employees when answering the phone was to give callers more than what they asked for and to play nice with each other. Everyone focused on the objective, not their personal convenience.

They found that this employee-based focus worked wonders! For the customers, their calls or e-mails were answered promptly, which translated to a consistently fun, productive, and inspiring experience when they called (www.conferencecallsunlimited. com).

Marketing Is Mostly Your Job

Before I can dive too far into the idea of a systematic marketing training program for your staff, I've got some bad news. No amount of training for your staff will help if you don't take responsibility for owning the marketing function in your business. You've probably come to realize that your staff will do as you *do* more readily than as you *say*.

The only way you can sell your internal clients—your staff— is if they recognize that you actually believe in and enact what you are selling. What have you done to really light their fire about what your company does, about how it is different, about the unique value you can bring to a service relationship?

So now that you know who the first target market is, your marketing purpose needs to get out there and start pounding the aisles, cubicles, break rooms, and conference tables looking for prospects who are just dying to be sold on the vision you have for the business.

If you meet resistance to this notion, it is because you have not made it a priority in the past, and people will always resist change. The key is that you make sure they understand that this isn't just another chapter from the latest business book you read. You must make the newfound emphasis on marketing an expectation and a requirement.

Create a Marketing Roundtable

While the primary marketing function may necessarily fall to you or some other person in your organization, you need to raise the level of marketing awareness systematically through focus, emphasis, and education.

One tool that many small businesses have discovered is

something I call a marketing roundtable. A marketing roundtable is a formal internal committee that meets to review and move marketing decision and actions forward. Part of this roundtable's responsibility is to also raise the overall level of internal marketing awareness.

Routinely Educate

The only way to keep the internal marketing message alive is to keep the message in view through routinely scheduled education practices. Every member of your staff must receive an orientation in the foundational marketing steps presented earlier in this book:

- *Your ideal target client description.* They must fully be able to picture who you work with and who you want to work with. From a practical standpoint, this will make them much more prepared to spot a potential new client.
- *Your marketing purpose.* What would it mean if they really understood and then found a way to connect their purpose to this?
- *Your Talking Logo.* Each staff member should be able to use this tool by connecting their function in the business to the ultimate marketing function.
- *Your Core Message.* This is everyone's Core Message.
- *Your marketing kit.* Your marketing kit provides so much information that it is likely to become one of your best hiring tools.

Part of the Hiring Process

Make marketing education and the emphasis on marketing part of your hiring process.

Put It on Business Cards

What if everyone had a supplemental title that addressed marketing functions? Think "vice-president of operations and customer service fanatic."

Employee Manual

Make your marketing Core Message and story a chapter in the employee manual. Put your marketing materials in your employee manual.

Quarterly All-Staff

Hold quarterly all-staff meetings, and allow your marketing roundtable members to share current marketing initiatives and results. Ask one member of your staff to deliver a presentation on one element of your marketing kit. This will take some pushing on your part, but people learn best by teaching. Keep at it!

Talking Logo Practice

I find that each staff member will connect to the idea of a Talking Logo in different ways. For some, using the company version will be uncomfortable because it may not feel authentic, depending upon their job. A printing press operator may not be able to deliver the exact same Talking Logo as the sales manager. It's vital that each member of your team have a Talking Logo that allows them to tap the marketing message but feels right for them.

Break your team up and facilitate some sessions that will help them create a "company approved" Talking Logo, and then help them practice using it.

Picture this: Your head of operations is at a cocktail party, and someone asks him what he does for a living, and instead of this: "I'm the head of operations for a small electrical contractor," he utters these words: "I make home builders look brilliant."

Or what if a field technician was confronted with a problem and instead of passing that problem on, she saw to it that the problem was addressed? *Then* she called the client back and made sure he was happy and offered to send the client some movie passes for his trouble.

Telephone Training

The telephone is often the portal to the prospect world for the small business. Everyone who answers the telephone for your organization should be trained to do it in a manner that represents and communicates your Core Message. This may require a script, practice, patience, and a zero tolerance policy, but it's that important.

External Marketing Training

Often, small businesses must rely on a series of contractors or vendors to deliver the results their clients expect. For instance, an office furniture dealer uses an external installation staff, or an advertising agency uses a courier service to deliver proofs to a client.

Guess what? Those outside or external partners are performing a marketing function on your behalf, no matter what the logo on their shirt says. While your clients may allow you some leeway due to the circumstances, they won't put up with shoddy service or bad manners consistently.

Kevin Lankford, The Authentic Success Coach, feels that the biggest aid to his business has been organization through documentation. He has developed his own operations manual that explains on a step-by-step basis the objectives for his business. The manual is broken down according to Administrative, Sales and Marketing, and Production tasks.

The manual also includes a page called "This is how we do

it." It's a step-by-step guide for those times when he needs to hire external help. It's better than a to-do list!

It's imperative that you choose vendors and partners who share your definition of customer service, but you can and should take it one step further and include them in some formal training. In some cases, it can be as simple as outlining and communicating your expectations. Over time, this simple step will help you define and attract your ideal strategic partners and vendors.

I worked with a remodeling contractor that hosted quarterly meetings for subcontractors to present actual scenarios of how to handle situations that might occur on a job site. Expectations and processes were presented as well. In order to be considered for projects, the subcontractors had to attend these sessions. Field managers also graded each subcontractor on a set of performance expectations. This contractor was more performance sensitive than price sensitive. Needless to say, he attracted only the subs, and his business and profits soared.

Your New Marketing Business Kick-Off

If you've been in business for any amount of time and have finally decided, by virtue of reading this book, to commit to a marketing point of view for your business, your staff will be in for a shock. After all, you're changing the rules.

I have found that one of the best ways to accomplish the kick-off of your new marketing attitude is to make a big deal out of the announcement of your marketing training and education program. Depending on how much change you are prepared to ask your team to make, you should do everything you can to make sure they realize you are serious about this initiative.

You should consider holding an all-staff meeting off-site, for a designated period of time. Create a packet of materials, hype the event, and build an air of expectation. Make sure that you have completed most of the steps presented previously in this book so that you can "roll-out" the new look, new message, new logo, and new attitude in a stunning way. Treat this meeting as one of your most important sales calls for your new marketing business. Think balloons, T-shirts, cake, and logo apparel. Paint the new picture, outline the new future, present the new expectations, and commit to the next steps in this education process. Most of all, commit the resources to launch powerfully.

A Marketing Board of Directors

Another very powerful marketing education tool is a marketing board of directors. Many times small business owners feel they don't have access to strategic thinking resources, that much of the work within their marketing world is tactical in nature. The focus is spent on writing the ad, ordering the list, or working with the designer.

A marketing board of directors, made up of members who can offer a strategic perspective to your marketing business, can be a great way to get outside advice to help drive your marketing decisions. Create a board mixed with clients, vendors, partners, and a community member or two, and ask them to commit to a quarterly meeting with the intent of reviewing and commenting on your marketing plans and progress.

The benefits to this approach make it well worth the small amount of work it may require to recruit your board. Clients of mine have found that a marketing board offers several benefits:

- It gives them someone to hold them accountable—most notably, the quarterly report of results drives them to focus on achieving goals.

- It provides creativity beyond what the owner or staff could muster while working in the business.
- It creates a loyal group of external champions—board members often feel compelled to champion a business they become this deeply connected with.

A Game Worth Winning

Finally, find a way to turn your marketing into a game. If you can find ways to motivate everyone in the organization to help grow the enterprise, think of what a machine you could create. This motivation may take the form of goal setting, score keeping, incentives, and a significant commitment on your part.

If you find that you have people that don't want to play the game, do them a favor—let them seek other opportunities. Let your folks know from day one that they are part of the marketing team.

Action Steps

1. Create a list of people who could serve on your marketing board.
2. Complete the core marketing exercises in the first six chapters.
3. Plan an all-staff marketing kick-off.

Part II

The Duct Tape Lead Generation Machine—Turning Stickiness into a System That Works for You

(Help Them *Contact and Refer* You More!)

Think back to high school physics class for a moment—if you can. (I didn't do so well in that class, so I'll simplify!) We learned in the laws of physics that it takes a whole bunch of force to get something moving, but once you get it moving, you can keep it moving with less force. To apply this lesson to marketing, think of force as exposure.

One of the great ways to build momentum is through lots of exposure. And for the small business without a big, fat budget, exposure is delivered by coming at your market from many angles. You can't rely on one form of advertising or communication to get the job done. You need to deliver a Core Message through as many vehicles as you possibly can.

You must have a referral promotion, an advertising promotion, a public relations promotion, a strategic partner promotion, an e-mail promotion, a speaking promotion, a writing promotion, a newsletter promotion . . . you get the point, right?

Again, think of it as applying layers of duct tape. The more you apply, the stronger the hold. In the next four chapters I will reveal powerful ways to generate leads by carefully integrating and layering various advertising, public relations, and referral marketing tactics to create tremendous momentum in your marketing system.

How will you know you've pulled off momentum? When you walk into a prospect's office to make a sales presentation and they are already sold. Marketing momentum does away with the need to sell!

By implementing the advice and strategies in the first section of the Duct Tape program, you have now built a solid foundation for helping your ideal clients *know*, *like*, and *trust* you more. Along the way, you've learned a thing or two about the basics of truly sticky marketing, so now it's time to move from the foundation of a sticky business identity to create a system of lead generation that will take stickiness to a whole new level. Just like adding new layers of duct tape, by adding the strategies in the coming chapters you will solidify your marketing efforts firmly in the direction of creating clients and customers. That's what you've been waiting for now, isn't it?

Chapter Eight
Run Advertising That Gets Results

Why Most Advertising Doesn't Work

Small business owners are often leery of advertising. And that's because it's expensive and it doesn't work, right? Well, not exactly. Most small businesses, particularly those adept in the art of Copycat Marketing, run advertising that rarely produces results and, therefore, conclude that advertising is not a good way to generate leads or sales.

Advertising, when viewed properly, can be a very effective way to grow your business. In fact, when a small business lands on an effective advertising promotion, few things can match it for quickly generating a flood of new business. The key lies in understanding what advertising really is, or at least what it should be.

Advertising is salesmanship in print. I'm certainly not the first to define advertising as such, but I think that definition fits perfectly and should help clarify how to use advertising as a lead generation tool. So think about that. If advertising is your salesperson in print, what does your ad need to do to be an effective salesperson?

The Image Salesperson

Pick up most any publication and take a look at the advertising. Almost every ad you will find is something that I will call *image advertising*. In other words, the ad does nothing to motivate me to act, it simply attempts to present an image that represents the company and provides me with some basic contact information should I accidentally choose to contact the company because I have nothing better to do with my time. Some people, even ad reps, refer to this as *awareness advertising*. Sure, people do need to be aware of your existence, but is that enough? Is that what you want from your highly paid salesperson?

Imagine hiring a salesperson, dressing him in a fine blue suit, red tie, and polished shoes and sending him out to a prospect with a sales pitch that goes something like this: "Hi, I'm Ted. Betcha you didn't know that we have a big fat logo, oh, and we've been in business for twenty years, and we know what you need—here's my phone number. Call when you want us to come out and sell you something."

> From this day forward, do not even think about placing an ad unless you are placing a direct response ad.

I know that sounds a bit absurd, but that's about all you accomplish when you run image or awareness style advertising. Oh, and you also spend a lot of money too. Major corporations may be able to afford to pump lots of dollars into image advertising as they attempt to position their brands, but I'm guessing that since you bought a book called *Duct Tape Marketing*, you can't.

Your ads, your salesperson in print, must stand up and represent your best sales presentation times one thousand. So, how do you do that? From this day forward do not even think about placing an ad unless you are placing a direct response ad.

A direct response ad is, as the name implies, an ad intent on generating a very specific response or action. Many people are familiar with the term *direct response* as it applies to direct mail, but I'm asking you to apply the concept to the entire category of advertising. This includes print ads, radio ads, television ads, Yellow Pages ads, and, yes, direct mail ads.

A direct response ad, like a good salesperson, gets an appointment (attention), goes out there and makes a case for your business, offers proof that you can provide a solution, shares facts, and makes a very specific offer or defines next steps. Sounds a bit like a sales call, doesn't it?

But now you may be thinking, that's great, but to do all that I'm going to need to buy full page ads, and who can afford that? That is the dilemma, isn't it? You can't possibly tell your prospect everything they need to know in the space of a two-by-three-inch ad, can you? But what if that's the only ad you can afford?

Introducing Two-Step Direct Response Advertising

As the name implies, two-step advertising is simply a form of advertising that motivates readers or listeners to take a step or action (Step One) that essentially signals that you have their permission to begin marketing to them (Step Two). Step One by the prospect signals Step Two by you, and the marketing dance is begun.

This powerful process is set into motion by advertising that offers the reader free or low-cost information or services only. The sole intent of a two-step ad is to generate a qualified response or action—not to make a sale. When you offer a free how-to report, tip sheet, industry insider scoop, or other valuable information, you start the process of building a relationship, building trust, with your prospects.

Once a suspect responds to your ad, you now know that you have a highly qualified lead and one that, through your special report filled with lots of reasons to hire you, already knows a great deal more about what makes you different from everyone else in your industry.

Step One: run ads that offer the reader a free report, sample, or something of high perceived value.

Step Two: send the report to all who respond and market to this group like crazy.

When someone responds to your two-step ad, you have a lead that is ready to receive your full marketing kit. (Remember that from chapter 5?) Essentially, you have a lead that has said they want you to educate them. In some cases, you may find yourself with a lead that is already sold on your product or service before you ever really contact them.

Lewis Green of L&G Business Solutions attributes most of his business growth to direct advertising that employs a two-step process. First, he mails a seven-page, detailed marketing letter. He follows-up by sending a postcard several weeks later.

He uses both his own mailing list, built through networking, and purchased lists that are narrowly targeted. The marketing letter offers a guarantee, details about the results he can produce, testimonials, brief case studies, a client list, and a menu of services (www.l-gsolutions.com).

The reason two-step advertising is so effective is that it allows you to make a very compelling offer to your suspects, in very simple terms, with little to no risk on their part. The typical two-step ad asks readers to visit a Web site or call a phone number and exchange some basic contact information in return for what they hopefully perceive is very valuable information

The two-step concept has been around for ages. In fact, I venture to say that you have probably responded to an ad much like this at some point, but few small businesses apply this very proven advertising approach to their lead generation efforts. Any business, no matter what the product or service, can create and offer some sort of free information or trial sample.

When it comes right down to it, most small businesses are really in the information business. Properly serving your customers requires exchanging information, even if that information is simply showing a customer how to use your product. Documenting and sharing the information you communicate, use, distribute, or otherwise employ to serve your clients just makes perfect sense.

The Benefits of Two-Stepping

- For the most part, when you run a two-step ad, you can think in terms of much smaller ads and much smaller ad costs. If all you are attempting to do with your ad is get the reader's attention and lead her to a Web page or toll-free number, you may be able to run a much smaller ad. Let your free report do the educating.

- The entire fulfillment process for your free report can be automated, leaving you the time and energy to focus only on prospects that have proven they need and want what you have to offer.

- Two-step advertising is very trackable. Every time someone calls or visits a Web page to get a report, you can track exactly where that lead came from. This is a great tool for advertising negotiations and allows you to fine-tune your advertising budget.

- Because the value to the reader is very high and the risk is very low, you will generate a much higher rate of response to your ads, and, if educated properly, many more of those who respond and become prospects will eventually become clients.

- Your sales calls will be much more productive, as your prospects will have been properly exposed to what you do, how you do it, and what makes your approach so valuable. This educational approach to your advertising generally leads to a much shorter sales cycle.
- You can effectively eliminate the need for cold calling. By producing and promoting your free report, your sales team will find a renewed source of leads that are highly qualified and at least partially sold.
- The use of special reports, teleseminars, articles, and how-to tip sheets in your marketing efforts will automatically help differentiate your business from others in your industry and move you and your firm to expert status.

What the Heck Should You Offer in Your Two-Step Ads?

You may recall that I introduced this idea of a free educational marketing report way back in chapter 5 as we discussed the marketing hourglass, but let's go into a bit more detail here.

The free information you offer can take many forms. The main thing you need to consider is that the information you are offering be perceived as valuable. If all you offer is a thinly veiled sales brochure, your efforts will suffer.

To develop or identify a good information product, think in terms of topics that will help your readers avoid the pain of paying too much, wasting their time, losing something they value, or encountering frustrating situations. It's just human nature that people seem very interested in topics that will help them avoid pain. So your information product could be titled this way:

- The Secrets of Hiring a Roofing Contractor Without Getting Burned

- The Legal Tax Cuts Your Accountant May Not Even Know About
- 101 Ways to Get More from Act Software
- What Your Pediatrician May Not Be Telling You about Car Seats
- 10 Surefire Methods to Help You Evaluate Your Auto Mechanic's Ethics
- How to Buy Everything at 50 Percent Off
- How to Squeeze Every Drop of Value from Your Attorney
- Professional Mover's Secrets to Packing Your Household Possessions So Nothing Gets Damaged
- 10 Must-Know Health Tips for People over 40
- How to Be Sure You Pay the Absolute Lowest Health Insurance Premium
- 10 Things You Must Know Before You Lease a Car
- How to Create a Flood of New Business in 7 Simple Steps

I am guessing that you can see that these titles all have a bit of drama associated with them. Your report title and subject need to get the prospect's attention and grab him quickly.

Up to this point, I have referred to this two-step advertising tool as a free report. Typically, this type of information product can take the form of a written eight-to-twelve-page document, often referred to as a white paper, which can be printed and mailed or housed on a Web site as a PDF document and automatically distributed upon request.

However, don't limit your thinking strictly to the white paper format. Often your message can be very compelling in a number of formats. This can take the form of a teleseminar, audio CD, workshop, recorded phone message, or e-mail series.

The teleseminar is a very interesting concept, as people are finding it harder and harder to get out of the office for seminars and workshops. With a teleseminar, you simply advertise your hot topic and allow people to sign up to call in through a conference setup and listen to your presentation. This can be a great, low-cost way to introduce your concepts and expertise to potentially large audiences.

Power Tip

Create a series of hot-topic teleseminars that can include information from other related industry folks (think in terms of other business owners or professionals that you would like to partner with), and interview these outside experts as part of your series. If you pick the right partners, you can use the series to cross-promote your business with the clients and prospects of your strategic partner. This is also a great way to expand your network of related professionals or even network with an industry leader that may otherwise not have known you existed. Do you see the referral potential of this strategy?

Most conference call companies also offer recording services as part of their package. Once you have the teleseminar recorded, you can reuse it on your Web site or as a promotional CD to ship to prospects who want more information.

If the thought of creating an eight-to-twelve page document, or even producing the content for a seminar, frightens you, then just rough out a good topic, including the eight to ten points that you know your readers need to know, and get a freelance writer to finish it up for you. You can easily find some very talented writers by posting your project needs on Web services such as www.elance.com.

Free vs. Paid

I have referred to the two-step information repeatedly as a free tool because there is often more interest in something that people can get for free. However, in some cases it may actually be better for you to attach a small price to your information product. Depending upon the nature of the information, some may perceive it to be of much greater value if they pay something for it. While this small cost approach will limit the overall number of respondents, generally those who pay for the information, even a token amount, will be highly qualified prospects.

A book, much like the one you are reading, can act as a low-cost tool to promote your business. A low-cost, introductory service that delivers a simple value and allows you to get a foot in the door can be an effective tool. You can conduct a number of teleseminars like those described above and package three or four with transcripts to create a very attractive, low-cost information product that firmly positions your business as an expert.

Sampling

Another way to attract suspects is to allow them to sample your product or service under no obligation. Take a cue from a typical Saturday afternoon in almost every grocery store in America. As you stroll the isles, pondering what to make for dinner, you are tempted by a variety of sample treats all aimed at enticing you to try, and then purchase, the jumbo pack of the treat.

If you have a unique product or service, you may benefit by simply getting it, in some form, into the hands of your suspects. Your free information may come in the form of a sample pack or valuable audit or evaluation.

Offer Value

I can't say this enough. Offer something of value and people will respond. As you create your two-step information product, you should actually assign a dollar value of worth to it. If you offer a workshop, make sure that it is a $79 value. If you offer sample packs, free reports, audio seminars, or evaluations, assign a value to them and communicate the value of your offer in your advertising.

And, of course, overdeliver on the stated value. Don't worry about giving too much away. Depending on what you have to offer, you will only enhance your status as an expert when you demonstrate, through your information products, that you do indeed know what you are talking about. The best news of all, though, is that most of those you compete with won't offer anything like this. Do I need to bring up the whole trust thing again? So let's recap the two-step approach:

- Create a free information product that your target market would see as a valuable read or listen.
- In all of your advertising, promote the free or low-cost information product only.
- Capture the names, addresses, and e-mails of those who request the report.
- Follow up with those leads.

If you take this advice to heart, everything about how you market your business will change. Finding new business will become a much more rewarding and valuable experience.

A Word about Cold-Calling

I know, I know, using this system, you shouldn't ever need to cold call; but if you do, do it this way. Call up those prospects on your list and instead of trying to convince them to give you five minutes of their time a week from Tuesday, offer them the address of your power-packed, free info.

Hi, this is Bob Smith with XYZ consulting. If I had a ten-page report that shows business owners thirteen little known ways to dramatically cut their costs, would you be the person I should send that to?

If you've done your homework on your list, then a call like this will be well received. Send the report and follow up in a week or so. Your prospecting time will be much more productive.

Elements of an Effective Two-Step Direct Response Ad

As I stated previously in this chapter, a direct response ad is salesmanship in print multiplied. Your ad can reach thousands of prospects at a time, but remember that the ad is read by each prospect one at a time. So write your ad as though you are talking to one prospect sitting across the desk from you.

> **The purpose of an ad is to convey a message and make an offer. I'm not saying that your ads should be ugly, but I'll take simple and ugly with the right message over breathtaking but "not really even sure what you sell" every day.**

Like a good sales call, your ad should lead readers through a series of steps toward the logical conclusion that they must contact you to receive their free report. From there the act of turning this lead into a client becomes a somewhat predictable game—but we'll go into much greater detail on that point in a later chapter. It's the message that counts.

One of the things that often hampers the effectiveness of an ad is the aspiration to make ads look pretty. Or worse, make them pretty and make them clever. Know this: your prospects are probably not coming to you to be entertained. This is a tough one for some to swallow, particularly those who come from industries where their peers place a high value on image or looking good (you know who you are).

The purpose of an ad is to convey a message and make an offer. I'm not saying that your ads should be ugly, but I'll take simple and ugly with the right message over breathtaking but "not really even sure what you sell" every day. The most effective small business ads focus on grabbing and keeping your readers' attention, offering them a host of benefits, and inspiring them to do something—*one* thing. At times this isn't always art school elegant, but a confused prospect is no prospect at all.

Single Most Intended Response

Don't try to do too much with your ads. Don't try to explain every possible service or combination of services or divisions of service that exist. It's tempting to think that if you spend the money on the ad, you want to get your money's worth. Of course when you take this approach, the opposite is what generally occurs.

In all of your ads, you must decide the one thing you want your readers to know or do the most and then focus every word in your ad in directing them to that and only that.

The Duct Tape Marketing Ad Formula

Okay, now that we've swept away all the bad ad stuff, let's get at that art of crafting an effective ad for your business.

You should make an attempt to include the following five elements in each ad you create: headline, benefits, proof, offer, and call to action. In some cases, for instance a classified ad, you may not have the space for each, or you may need to combine elements.

Headline

The headline is the heart and soul of an effective ad. Every ad needs a headline—it's that simple. Think of this as the audition for your ad. When someone is flipping through a magazine, the decision to stop and read your ad is made in one to two seconds or less. Your ad must grab them by the throat, and a powerful headline is the only way to do that.

You should spend more time writing headlines for your ads than any other element. That's how important it is. Did I mention that every ad starts with a headline? This includes ads that don't typically have headlines—such as phone directory ads and sales letters.

The best headlines contain some aspect of the offer you intend to make or specifically name the prospect the ad is targeting.

> *Free report reveals legal tax cuts that most accountants don't even know about.*

> *Headache sufferers finally get relief from pain—free report provides little-known steps.*

Benefits

Sell your report, the action you want to reader to take, by pointing out the benefit of reading the report. "You will finally know when . . ." Don't talk about what is in the report; explain what problem the report solves, what readers will get or have once they know this content.

Proof

Tell readers about someone who made a brilliant discovery or avoided a terrible mistake because of the information you are about to share with them. Testimonial quotes from happy clients often fill this need.

Offer

Make them the offer of your free report. Depending upon your particular business, your offer can be a free class or special give-away or contest, but your ad must give a reason to act.

Call to Action

Tell them what to do now. Make it easy for them to contact you or take the next step. Offer several ways for them to take advantage of your offer. Give them the option to visit a Web page or call a toll-free number.

As you can see, following this formula will make for a copy-heavy ad, and that's just fine. If you compose a headline that gets the attention of readers and pulls them in, then the more copy, the better. There is very little value in having your logo dominate your ad.

If you are offering a free report or audio CD, then an image of the report can add to the sense of value. Try to strike a balance between design and content, but make sure that the content is king. Remember to state the dollar value of your free report.

What Forms of Advertising Make the Most Sense for Your Business?

This is one of those questions that can only be answered in a very frustrating way. The best form of advertising for your business is the one or ones that work. It is nearly impossible in the context of this work to tell you exactly where you should place your advertising, as every community, industry, and market segment has different advertising opportunities.

You should, however, look at your advertising from a return on investment (ROI) point of view. You want the greatest bang for your buck when it comes to advertising. So often advertisers can't tell you what the return on their advertising is. One of the greatest things about the two-step approach outlined in this chapter is that it offers a chance to understand exactly how your advertising is performing. Three principles come into play when trying to analyze your best advertising ROI.

1. *Target your ads.* Does the advertising you are considering deliver a very high amount of your target market? Most advertising is priced based on readership, viewers, subscribers, or market share. If your ideal target market only makes up 5 percent of the base readership of a magazine you are considering, you still pay for the other 95 percent.

2. *Test your ads.* You can and should test your ads on a small scale whenever possible to help determine the effectiveness of the ad itself as well as the chosen advertising medium, such as a magazine or newspaper. Once you find ads and advertising vehicles that produce results, you can begin to explore ways to expand your advertising message into other vehicles.

   The idea is to find something that works and then test ways to beat the ad that works. Your best performing ad is known as your control ad. Stick with this control ad as long as it is working.

   Advertising is a repetition game. One-shot ads in publications or on air are not going to bring you the ultimate response that repeated exposure to your market brings. For this reason it is essential that you test and find a message or offer that generates a predictable response. (Advertising is often discounted when you can commit to a once-a-month ad as opposed to a one-time ad.)

3. *Track your ads.* In order to effectively test and evaluate the ROI of your ads, you need a system to track where a lead comes from. If you only run one ad at a time, this could be a

pretty simple system; but when you have ads placed in numerous publications, running on the radio, on the Internet, and through direct mail, it is helpful to devise a system to code and track your responses. There are some very powerful tracking software programs and Web-based applications that make tracking online responses to an ad a snap. You simply code every ad or mailing with a different URL that identifies the ad and then view your results.

Another form of advertising tracking comes in the form of telephone-based tracking systems. These systems allow you to place different phone numbers in your ads and then track specifics about each call, coming from each number. All of the calls are ultimately forwarded to your main number, but these systems can produce feature-rich reports about the results of each call. This is an attractive option for businesses such as home service providers that rely on phone calls for a great deal of their business.

You can also adopt a low-tech approach by coding direct mail ads with different key codes or extension numbers and then track the responses for each. I've even had clients ask the reader to call and ask for a series of fictitious names as a tracking device.

You can, and should, also run what are called A/B split tests where you may have identical offers sent to two different lists or run on two different radio stations to test which performed the best. You may also do an A/B split test by sending one half of a list a mailing with one headline and the other half of the list with a completely different headline. Track the results, and go to work beating the one that had the best results by changing and testing some other element such as price or offer against the winner.

Finally, at the very least, ask your prospects, and even your Web site visitors who fill out a form to request a free report, where they heard about you. Just tape this question near the phone of everyone in the office and tally the results often.

The Advertising Research That Really Matters

Here is one final note on determining what media to explore for your advertising purposes. Advertising sales reps will tell you all kinds of glowing demographic information about their publication or station and the millions upon millions of hot prospects that you can expect when you advertise with them. Now I'm not saying they are making this stuff up, but the only thing that really matters is whether or not your target market reads, listens to, or subscribes to the medium.

One of the best things you can do as you try to determine whether to test one vehicle over another is ask your existing clients what they read and where they get their information. You will be amazed how often publications will rise to the top of your list when you hear that they are more valuable than another to your ideal client. This is particularly true with free subscription industry-type publications. In some cases, these publications can have very impressive subscriber numbers but nobody really reads them.

Another potentially powerful advertising research tip is to pick out a handful of ads from noncompetitive businesses that currently advertise in an advertising medium you are considering. Then simply call these advertisers, business owner to business owner, and ask them how happy they are with their return from the ad. Beware if none of those you call can speak directly about results from the ad.

Creating a Small Business Advertising Plan

Beware: Media Sales Reps Ahead

One of the most obnoxious types of salefolks out there is the media sales rep. (Like all generalizations, this one is occasionally wrong.) When you begin to build your media plan, you will encounter salespeople from every media outlet in town, and each and every one of them will try to convince you that your business cannot survive without the special they are running this week.

Please accept the information they can pass along, and then ignore them. I know this advice won't win me any friends in the media sales arena, but unfortunately some in the industry teach members to tell you anything they can to get the sale.

You now know more about marketing than most media sales folks, and you certainly know more about your business. Use this knowledge to make your advertising decisions, and be very wary of the stunning demographic information and graphs and charts media salespeople produce.

To get started with your small business advertising plan, I suggest that you contact the television stations, radio stations, newspapers, magazines, and other media outlets that you feel serve your target market and ask them to send you a "media kit." An advertiser's media kit consists of a description of the medium, demographics of readers or listeners, editorial calendars, and advertising rates. This collection is where you start to analyze opportunities to promote your business through advertising.

Most small businesses can create a simple spreadsheet to log the majority of the possible advertising opportunities. This spreadsheet should consist of the name of the medium, contact information, distribution or number subscribers, cost of an ad, and a calculation of the cost of the ad per 1,000 listeners, readers, or viewers. This last number is known in the ad world as cost per thousand or CPM. (M being the Roman numeral for 1,000.)

When comparing each of the advertising mediums that follow, it is important to understand that most advertising is sold on a cost per thousand basis (CPM) and that when you are trying to compare pricing it's very important to understand the CPM of an ad when evaluating one against another.

A low-cost ad that doesn't really reach anyone may actually be more expensive in the big picture than an ad that is more expensive per insertion but reaches a greater audience.

Typical Small Business Advertising Opportunities—Pros and Cons

The following is a list of the typical advertising mediums available to the small business in most communities. While this list may not be exhaustive, it does cover the primary advertising tools that you can employ in your lead generation work. I am admittedly a bit biased toward several of these but try to offer the pros and cons that each may bring your business.

Network television. While television advertising offers very high impact, it is possibly the most expensive advertising buy and becoming less and less effective for the small business with the advent of so many other forms of television and television-like media.

Cable television. Cable television does offer more ability to target certain market niches or demographics with specialty cooking, gardening, furniture building, and sports-only type programming.

Recently, a new breed of television ad agency has cropped up that allows local small advertisers to choose an industry specific, professionally produced ad, customize it, and place a media buy all in a matter of minutes. The most successful is a California company called Spot Runner (www.spotrunner.com). The lower cost associated with this approach is making television more attractive to local small businesses.

Radio. It's a good way to target with the right station. Every station has a pretty narrow demographic set of listeners. Radio is also a good way to get repetition in your message as listeners tend to be loyal both to stations and parts of the day. Radio is a very good tool for a sale of promotion announcement.

Don't forget public radio. Public radio does not have the same commercial clutter of a typical radio station and offers a very strong demographic of upper management, well-educated, higher income listeners. No ads are available, only sponsorship mentions that have become increasingly advertiser friendly.

Local newspapers. This is a good choice for many retail businesses, but it's a medium that is increasingly ineffective for most other forms of business due to a lack of targeting. Some weekly newspapers can be well-read in certain communities and allow you to connect to certain demographic groups.

Almost every major city also has what is known as an alternative newspaper. These publications generally focus on entertainment and can be an effective way to reach a fairly defined demographic.

Business newspapers. In some communities these publications can be good ways to communicate with business-only markets. It is very important to have a way to measure results.

Magazines. Magazine advertising is probably the riskiest choice for a small business as the cost of advertising is generally significant and the time before an ad may appear can be as much as ninety days. However, magazines do offer high impact exposure for some industries and even national publication like *TIME*, *Fortune,* and *Newsweek* offer regional advertising options. This kind of ad should only be run after you have an ad that you have fully tested. The image impact of a full-page ad in a national publication can be valuable but must be weighed against the cost.

Yellow Pages. The good news about the Yellow Pages is that when someone picks it up they are typically looking to buy what you sell. The bad news is that when they get to your ad it is surrounded by all of your competitors. Yellow Pages will continue to lose effectiveness to the Internet alternatives. If your ad appears in a Yellow Pages directory, it is imperative that you offer the reader a compelling reason to call you other than to get a price quote comparison.

Outdoor. Billboards have limited appeal for most small businesses and certainly must be run in conjunction with other forms of advertising, but they can be very effective as a direct response vehicle if your business is location based. "Exit here for great food" is a call to action available on a billboard. Billboards are also a great tool to announce a new product or enhance a trade show.

Direct mail. From a targeting standpoint, direct mail is likely the best option for most small businesses. You can purchase very targeted mailing lists and fully control who receives your message. Small tests can help you quickly determine what works and what doesn't.

Telemarketing. Almost completely ineffective as a lead generation tool, telemarketing still can offer impact when used to follow up other forms of marketing such as a direct mail campaign.

Internet. Depending upon the type of business and scope of operation, this form of advertising offers some interesting and ever changing opportunities. As Internet surfers continue to use the Web as the new phone book, local Internet advertising options will flourish.

Pay-per-click advertising (PPC) ads, run on Web sites and sold based on a click, have grown into a major form of local advertising. Google, Yahoo, MSN, and AOL all offer the ability for any business to bid on specific search terms in an effort to attract Web surfers to a classified type ad. Ads can be targeted to specific local terms and geographic locations.

PPC also offers a tremendous opportunity to test messages and headlines very quickly and inexpensively. An ad placed on a system like Google AdWords can start appearing in a matter of hours after it is placed. The system also allows you to test multiple ads. Each ad and ad response is automatically tracked. In a couple of days of testing and at a very low cost, you may be able to determine that one headline gets far better response than another. While not every business can rely on PPC advertising to generate sufficient leads, it is one of my favorite testing grounds regardless of where you plan to run your ads.

Neighborhood. Almost every community has coupon ad packs, flyer distribution services, and other co-op type opportunities that may make sense for your business. Again, the question is always who does it reach, not how cheap is it.

Create your own advertising vehicles. Bob Hamilton Plumbing created some yard signs during an election and convinced some customers to put them in their yard at the height of the electioneering cycle. These signs promoted "Bob Hamilton for Plumber." They were cute and likely generated some positive buzz.

I've long considered the yard-sign idea to perhaps be more powerful than the casual, one-time use might imply. What if you were to find a few well-placed homeowners—that would mean on high traffic residential through streets—and offered to buy some advertising in their yard? The stipulation would be that they would agree to place a sign promoting your business or service in their yard and to leave it there.

I know some of the homeowner association types might be rolling their eyes, but like anything you do, if you take care to select homes that have side yards and maybe only use a thirty-day term, who knows? This is an ideal approach for home services folks—window cleaning, landscaping, plumbing, HVAC, and the like.

Now let's expand our thinking a bit. What about delivery vehicles, statement stuffers for complimentary businesses, printed trash bags, recycling bins, pizza delivery boxes? There's really no limit to this idea of creating your own advertising vehicles.

Strategic partnerships. While this isn't really an advertising medium, I want to mention it here. There is quite likely a host of companies that serve your very same target market that could be enticed to participate in some form of joint marketing. This can take the form of mailings that endorse your product or service, cooperative marketing efforts, or simply distributing the marketing materials of other related businesses. I'll cover this idea in greater detail in the chapter on referrals.

Duct Tape Marketing Chapter Resources

The following list of Web sites may help you locate various local media outlets in your community and across the country.

Television
   Find TV - http://www.tvfind.us/
   Newslinkhttp://newslink.org/broad.html
   Spotrunner – http://www.spotrunner.com

Radio
   Radio locator - http://www.radio-locator.com/
   Radio directory - http://www.radiodirectory.com/
   Newslink - http://newslink.org/broad.html
   Public Radio - http://www.radio-locator.com/
   cgibin/finder?format=pub&s=R&sr=Y

Newsprint
   Hometown News - visit http://www.hometownnews.com/
   Newslink - http://newslink.org/news.html

State Newspaper Associations can place ads in many newspapers at one time.

Business Newspapers

Newslink - http://newslink.org/biznews.html

BizJournals - http://www.bizjournals.com/

Classified Ad Networks

Nationwide - www.nationwideadvertising.com/

Magazines

Newslink - http://newslink.org/mag.html

Wikipedia list - http://en.wikipedia.org/wiki/List_of_United_States_magazines

Outdoor (Billboards)

Outdoor Advertising Association - http://www.oaaa.org/members/roster/

Action Steps

1. Contact every media outlet in your market and request a media kit to start comparing different forms of advertising.
2. Look to your clients and their problems and frustrations to create one or more "hot topic" information products to offer your market.
3. Ask your current clients what publications they read to help determine where you should consider placing your advertising.

Chapter Nine
Direct Mail Is an Ideal Target Medium

Why Is Direct Mail an Ideal Target Medium?

So, I'm a homebuilder, building homes in the posh new Platypus Creek development, and I get two pieces of mail from a home stereo equipment provider.

One has a headline that says: "We have the home audio products your customers want."

The other provider says: "Homebuyers in Platypus Creek are demanding whole-house stereo—we'll show you how to profit from that demand."

Now, in this scenario, who would the homebuilder consider calling first? In this chapter you will discover how to tap into the power of one of my favorite forms of advertising for the small business—direct mail.

The reasons I like direct mail are pretty simple, but it all leads back to my prevailing principles when it comes to analyzing any form of advertising.

1. Does it allow you to specifically target your Ideal Prospect?
2. Does it provide a high return on investment?

Properly executed, direct mail offers a resounding yes to both of the above questions.

Few advertising mediums are targeted enough to offer the small business a high enough return on investment, but the primary reason I believe direct mail is the best choice for most small businesses is that you can start very small, test very quickly, and easily expand your efforts when you have a winner.

My advice to almost every one of my clients is to start with direct mail campaigns, focus on creating letters and offers that deliver a predictable response, and then, and only then, look to add other forms of advertising to expand and enhance your message. It is unreasonable to believe that a marketing message that does not pull any response in a direct mail letter will fair much better in a half-page ad in a newspaper. However, it is often the case that an offer that does well in direct mail will also do well in other forms of media.

Personalization Builds Trust

Another very compelling aspect of direct mail is the ability to personalize each and every piece sent. You naturally start by personalizing an envelope with the recipient's name and address, but other forms of variable printing allow you to address specific industry needs, provide geographic or neighborhood references, and list variables or headline variables such as headache sufferers vs. back pain sufferers.

There really is no end to the ways that you can creatively craft and personalize a direct mail piece to the point that it feels almost as though you created that one mailing just for the person who received it.

The Perfect Testing Platform

Direct mail also offers the best opportunity to test and track your advertising efforts. You can send as few as one hundred pieces of mail and assess with a certain degree of accuracy whether you stand a chance at meeting your lead generation goals. Further, you can send one hundred pieces of mail to a member of five different mailing lists, or with five different head-lines or offers, and get an immediate sense of which is the best. The low-risk, quick response, and low-cost nature of this form of testing makes it the best place to start your advertising efforts.

Donald Levin of Levin Public Relations in Larchmont, New York, uses what he calls the "Levin 10 Letters a Week" method to gain new business. First, he researches ten companies that he thinks he can provide profitable service to—profitable to the company and profitable to his business. He studies their Web sites and calls them to confirm the single best person to write to. Next, he writes all ten a concise letter that explains exactly what he can offer them and how and why they'll benefit. He closes the letter by saying when he will call to arrange a meeting.

Then he makes the calls. If he can't arrange a meeting, he finds out when he should call back (three months, six months, etc.). He keeps this information in a database and acts on it. The following Monday, he starts the whole process again (www.levinpr.com).

The List

While I have spent considerable time going on about the virtues of direct mail combined with the effective elements of an ad, I need to point out that one of the primary factors in the success or failure of a direct mail campaign is the list of recipients. We've already learned a lot about developing the right message, but if you mail the right message to the wrong people, your campaign is doomed to fail.

It is safe to say that you can purchase just about any mailing list or set of qualifications for a list that you could imagine. To develop your ideal mailing list, you should start by taking the work you did in developing your ideal target client and determine if you can buy a list of prospects that match that profile. The thought here is that if you do a good job of defining those who make up your ideal client, then you simply try to find more of them.

Mailing lists generally fall into two categories. Lists compiled from public records and lists of subscribers or enthusiasts. And you are going to go list shopping for both.

Simple lists "selects," such as companies in a certain metropolitan area with fewer than one hundred employees, can be acquired from a host of national list resources such as InfoUSA. These types of lists are often available at very reasonable rates.

Lists of subscribers of specific publications or buyers of specific services and products are also available but generally at substantially higher prices. A publication called the Standard Rates and Data Service (SRDS) lists over ten thousand mailing lists of all shapes and sizes available for rent. It is possible to find lists in the SRDS of credit card holding doctors who subscribe to hunting magazines. Okay, this particular example may not fit the bill, but I hope you see the potential here.

Mailing lists are sold on a cost per thousand basis, and most list owners have minimum list rental requirements, although I have found that many will waive the minimum to allow you to test a small amount of the list.

The Perfect Mailing List

Both the compiled list and the publication or purchaser list have value, but I believe the perfect mailing list is created by carefully merging several types of lists. To create your perfect mailing list, start by getting a list from a source like InfoUSA that meets your very strict demographic profile of your ideal client. Then find a list from a magazine or catalog from SRDS that demonstrates a purchasing or enthusiast behavior that matches your product or service and join the two lists to find prospects that reside on both lists. Anyone who appears on both lists is your ideal target. This way you narrow the list to only the most highly targeted suspects possible.

The trick is to identify some behavior or reason that someone would be on a certain list that would help better qualify them for your offering. (Remember the work we did back in chapters 1 and 2 on profiling your ideal client?) Let's say, for example, that you are a home remodeler. Would the fact that someone in your target market also subscribed to a publication all about upscale home design trends make them more likely to be a prospect for your service? Or how about a commercial insurance provider? Would a group of people that fit your demographic profile who also subscribe to a publication that keeps them up to date on worker's comp issues be potentially interesting to your marketing effort?

There is a generally accepted notion in direct mail circles that you can tell a great deal about what people think, how they act, and what they value based on what they buy. Your mailing list work is as much about understanding the culture of your ideal client as it is finding people who seem to belong on your list. It is very difficult to convince someone that they should spend money on what you have to offer. There are lots of businesses and individuals that need what you do, but when you analyze your suspect list, you need to focus on suspects that have demonstrated a past behavior that demonstrates that they value what you do or sell. This is essential to your mailing list research. If you sell consulting services, you need to look for companies that have demonstrated that they hire professional consultants. In this case, you can't afford to waste your time on businesses that don't seem to value professional service providers.

Your list cost may initially increase five-fold with the approach I described above, but since you will ultimately shrink the overall size of your list with this approach, you will mail far fewer prospects and receive a much higher return on each mailing. In some cases, you may have to expand your list selection a bit or resort to custom list building tactics to come up with a list of adequate size, but this practice will still deliver a better list in the end.

Doug Antonacci of Daddy O's Music Shack, a small music store in Springfield, Illinois, discovered a very low-cost, highly qualified list-building strategy. Each week, he goes online to view the classified ads in the local "penny paper" for bands or people selling used music gear (guitars, drums, etc.). Next, he copies their phone number on an Internet reverse look-up site and gets their mailing address. Then he mails them a flyer offering features and specials. The only real cost is a stamp and some printing. The best part is that he knows his mailing will get directly to a musician.

Your *Hot Suspect* List

Once you have done your list research and identified some number of qualified suspects, it is time to put these suspects into a contact database such as ACT. You can also simply save this list as a spreadsheet type of file, but it is best that you save your list in a way that will allow you to mail to the members of the list frequently and keep track of your response and follow-up activities. At this point, I suggest that you carve out a budget that allows you to mail to this list at least six times in the next six months.

The idea is to work with the number of suspects that your budget allows you to impact. By *impact*, I mean put your message in front of qualified suspects frequently enough to get noticed. Much of the lead generation tactics explained in the next two chapters will allow you to broaden your marketing efforts, but your initial hot suspect list should be manageable enough that you can flood them with your advertising offers and test and track messages frequently. Because advertising is often the biggest marketing "real dollar" expense, it is best if you can focus on this group in such a way that they will receive your messages six to eight times in a matter of months.

Depending upon your marketing goals and needs, a list of five hundred very qualified suspects may be more than enough to focus your entire marketing effort on. This decision starts with a determination of how much business you need to grow your business.

In some ways, your available budget may dictate the size of this initial group, but as you land upon successful campaigns, you can confidently expand this initial group to whatever size you can realistically serve. That's how powerful this narrow focus, direct mail approach is. Don't worry what the rest of the universe is doing. Set your marketing goals (how many new clients you want or need) and work with a group that is manageable enough that your direct mail campaign can begin to get their attention. Generally, it is better to mail the same five hundred suspects six times a year than to mail three thousand suspects only once.

A More Qualified List

It is always better to mail your marketing letters to the most qualified person within any company you have targeted. Mailing lists, even those from the most reputable companies, contain errors and out-of-date information. Your letter sent to the VP of Finance, who was fired three months ago, probably won't have much impact. Regardless of the size of your suspect list, it is well worth the time to call each company and locate the name of the person most qualified to purchase your products and services. Most company receptionists will provide a name when asked.

Martin Jelsema of Signature Strategies in Denver, Colorado, targets Colorado-based, high-tech companies about to launch a new product (because they need to brand the new offering). He uses the Sunday newspaper, help-wanted display ads to find companies needing design and test engineers, project managers, systems developers, etc.

Once he identifies the companies, he calls to find the top marketing person at these firms. On Monday, he mails each company a one-page letter suggesting he can help them "brand smart from the start," and that he has experience with high-tech product introductions. He also encloses a list of customers that he has previously assisted. Then he promises to call them later in the week to discuss their interest.

Because he identifies prospects with a need, demonstrates his professionalism in his personal letter, and establishes some credibility, he gets through to over 50 percent of those he writes and sets one or two appointments each week using this strategy (www.signaturestrategies.biz).

Your Sticky Sales Letter—Don't Leave Home without It

The very first advertising piece you must master is the sales letter. Your sticky sales letter is always a work in progress, but it is also the foundational piece for all of your advertising. To effectively launch your Duct Tape Marketing lead generation system, you must write and test a sales letter that generates enough leads to help move you toward your client and revenue goals.

You will eventually adapt components of this letter to use in other advertising vehicles and in other ad formats and mediums, but you can't pass go without this tool. The reason for the emphasis on this tool is fundamental. If you agree that direct mail is the most effective way to target your suspects, then a sales letter is the most effective way to turn those suspects into prospects and eventually into clients and referral sources.

Sticky Sales Letter Formula

Your sales letter should contain some element of each of following:

Headline. I've already covered this pretty thoroughly, but yes, even your sales letter needs a headline.

Your headline is the ad for your ad. Your headline must scream, "This letter is worth your time!" John Caples, who some consider the best copywriter ever (that's why the highest award a copywriter can win is called a Caples Award) said this about headlines:

> I spend hours on headlines—days if necessary. And when I get a good headline, I know that my task is nearly finished. Writing the copy can usually be done in a short time, if necessary. And that advertisement will be a good one, that is, if the headline is really a "stopper."

You must have a good story and a compelling offer in your body copy, but without a good headline, you don't stand a chance. Here are my three favorite headline starters:

- Ask a compelling question: "Do you know why . . ."
- State your offer: "Free report reveals 101 ways to . . ."
- Identify the target: "Mechanical engineers find that . . ."

Place your headline directly under the salutation in 18- or 24-point type.

State the problem. Let the reader know up front that you realize the problem they have and you understand the frustrations they are going through.

Stir up the problem. Draw a picture of what this problem is likely costing them in terms of money, time, frustration, or status.

Paint a hopeful future. Begin to reveal what life could be like or what it is like for some others like them.

Outline a solution. Show them that you have an idea how they can get relief. Layer on the benefits of your solution.

Answer objections. Address the objections that you know your prospects have posed in the past.

Make an offer. Offer your free report, workshop, CD, or other free or low-cost information product.

Create a call to action. Tell them why and how they should contact you to get this offer.

PS. Always end with a PS. Some people call this the second headline because after the headline, this is the most read part of a letter. Make sure that you restate your offer or chief benefit in a PS.

How to Get Your Letter Written

Here are my suggestions:

- Outline your letter using the formula.
- Write a rough draft in one sitting.
- Leave your letter alone for a day.
- Edit your letter for impact.
- Let a professional proof your letter for errors.
- Edit one final time for passion.

Copywriting Tips for Small Business Marketers

There are hundreds of books, courses, and Web sites that will help you become a better writer, and I recommend that you acquire and read as much as you can on the topic. You can't know enough about what I think is the master marketing skill. I now want to share a couple of tips that will immediately make you a better marketing writer.

Writing Is a Master Marketing Skill

Few things are sold without a prospect reading a written word or two. Business owners often ask me what they should be looking for in a marketing assistant, and I always tell them to find someone who can write. What I really mean is find someone who *will* write.

Many people claim that they are not good writers, and my take is that they simply don't write. In order to become a good writer, in order to use writing as a marketing skill, you must write. You can always have someone edit what you write, but it's the act of writing that starts the marketing ball rolling. (I know my editor friends out there wish I would take that editing advice.) Here's what I have found.

- Writing creates ideas. It's rarely the other way around. Many times I have no idea what I am going to write, but once I start, ideas just happen. What comes about is often far greater than anything I could have simply thought and then transferred to paper or screen.
- Writing helps you have something to say. The more you write, the better you will sell.
- Writing helps you listen more actively.
- Write speeches, write notes, write essays unrelated to your business.

Create a swipe file. This is just a file of letters and offers you receive and hang on to for ideas of what works and what doesn't work. You may want to get yourself on some direct mail order lists so that you receive some of the better sales letters out there. Three companies that send out very good direct mail letters are Nightingale Conant, Guthy Renker, and Bottom Line Publications.

Tell them why. If you are making a great offer in your copy, tell readers why you are making it. Don't assume they know. Tell them why you started your business, why you hope they fall in love with your products, why you are having a special sale, and why they should buy from you now.

> Your sales copy is meant to be a form of conversation with the reader. . . . Few things sound less sincere than when you try to be or sound like a really smart marketing person.

Write as you talk. This one always drives my English major readers crazy, but your sales copy is meant to be a form of conversation with the reader. Say what you believe, how you believe it, and you will connect with your reader. Few things sound less sincere than when you try to be or sound like a really smart marketing person.

Use subheadlines in your copy. Some readers will pour over your copy word for word; others will scan and jump to visual clues. Subheadlines that emphasis key logical points will help readers scan your letter.

Use quotes. Quotes, either from you or in the form of a testimonial, add another voice to your copy and allow for the conversation that you are trying to start.

Use active voice. I'm not trying to contradict "write as you talk," but active verbs can make your copy stronger. Have someone edit your copy looking specifically to change passive verbs to active ones. You will be amazed how this little edit can add punch.

Passive: "Just call day or night and your application will be picked up by our representative."

Active: "Just call day or night and our representative will pick up your application."

Tell stories. People love stories. Often even complicated ideas can be made simple through the use of a story. Talk about how your clients use your products or services. Talk about the day you realized that there was a need for what your offer.

Pretest Your Letter

Now that you've written your sticky sales letter, and you are happy with it, I recommend that you pretest it for readability. Here are a few tips to help you get this process started:

- Read your letter out loud to get a feel for how it sounds.
- Round up a twelve-year-old or two and see if they understand what you are offering.
- Show a copy to some of your best clients or prospects and ask for their input.

Your Sales Letter Package

Before you send your letter out there to your suspects, there are a couple of other considerations.

Outer Envelope

Theories abound on what works and what doesn't when it comes to getting your letter opened. Some of the variables in the mix have to do with the industry you are in, but as a rule, a simple #10 standard envelope, laser personalized, featuring your company logo, return address, and real stamp is the best package.

There are direct mail gurus out there who will tell you that you need clever teaser copy to get your mail opened, or you need to make your envelope look very official or like an invoice. While these ploys may indeed get your mail opened, they can backfire as they are a bit dishonest. Make your envelope look very important, and make it look as though the recipient is the only person you sent the letter to.

What Postage Rate?

Again, if you want your letter to look as though it was sent solely to the addressee, you are better off with a real stamp over a mailing permit. Depending upon the number of people you are sending your letter to, you may also find first class mail postage to be your best bet. No one can officially verify this, but studies have shown up to 25 percent of presort standard (bulk) mail does not reach its destination. This statistic, coupled with the fact that a bulk rate stamp signifies, well, bulk, makes first class stamps an attractive choice. (This, of course, is a variable that you can test!)

I guess this is the point where I must add a caveat. Everything I have said about the right way to prepare your direct mail package is wrong—if your testing can prove it so. I can't overemphasize the need to test many elements of your direct mail package. I have personally experienced 300 percent response increases by changing the headline of a letter.

Great Things Come in Small Packages

When comparing various forms of direct mail advertising, don't overlook the humble postcard. There are so many things to love about postcards, but low cost is one of the best. You can send an attention-getting message to a very targeted audience for under thirty cents each. This includes all of the benefits of using first-class mail. (Postage on a first-class letter is thirty-nine cents alone.)

I've already stated the value of repetition in your advertising. How about sending an attention-getting message, once a month, to your entire list of suspects and prospects for around $4.00 per lead, per year. Few things can compete with that potential ROI.

I love the direct mail letter for the heavy lifting, but postcards are a great way to supplement your primary offers and remind your current clients that you still care about them too. With a postcard, there is no envelope to open, so it is likely that your message will at least be seen, even if the reader only casually scans his or her mail.

The Use of Color

Digital printing has made color printing, even in small quantities, very affordable. There is plenty of scientific evidence to support the fact that color is more memorable, and the postcard offers a great opportunity to effectively use full color images in your advertising. As in all of your ads, you should use a short, impact-filled headline on your postcards. You only have a small space to get your message across. Grab your readers by the throat and make them sit up and listen.

A Couple of Other Uses for Postcards

While I really like postcards for generating prospects, there are many other great uses with your existing clients:

- Special client offerings
- Coupons

- News announcements
- New product announcements

Take your postcards to your next networking event. Everyone else is passing out business cards like crazy, and you can stand out by passing out your postcard ad with a dynamite offer on it.

There are certain postal regulations that relate to postcard mailings, so to be on the safe side check with the post office before you print.

The Post Office Is a Great Small Business Resource

In recent years the good old United States Post Office has discovered a little concept called customer service. Now, competition can do that to an organization, but the Post Office isn't just any organization, so I think it has responded nicely and turned itself into a valuable resource for small businesses.

One of the latest innovations is an online service that allows you to design business reply cards and envelopes (BRC and BRE) suitable for printing. The very precise process of creating these automated mailing tools used to be very tedious. Now you can visit ReplyMail.com and create one in several simple steps. You will need a permit for most, but you acquire that online as well. Business reply (the sender pays the return postage) can dramatically increase response rates for certain types of mailing promotions. I like to use it whenever I am trying to drive inquires for information or samples.

Don't Forget about Hand-Written Notes as a Direct Response Tool

Lori Chance of Destination Words in Portland, Oregon, uses a good, old-fashioned note card as one of her key marketing tools. She says, "They're fun to write, simple, and the receiver absolutely loves them!" On more than one occasion, she has gone to meet someone months after having sent them a card only to find the card still sitting on their desk or tacked to their bulletin board because "it makes them smile" (www.DestinationWords.com).

Lumpy Mail Always Gets Opened

When it comes to your gravy, lumps are bad. When it comes to getting your marketing message through the mailroom, past the gatekeepers, and onto your potential buyer's desk, lumps are just the ticket. While I do love the direct mail letter for small business lead generation, in the right circumstances I'm also particularly fond of something I call "lumpy mail." Lumpy mail is a direct mail piece or package with some dimension or lumps to it. A box is lumpy mail. A balloon arrangement, a kitten, and a hula hoop are all examples of a lumpy mail package. You name it. The point is, you just can't ignore a piece of lumpy mail.

Some prospects are next to impossible to reach with traditional mailings. So, sometimes you need to up the ante and make a real statement. A lumpy mail package screams, "Notice me! Open me!"

Lumpy mail is a piece of Duct Tape Marketing that Kandy Meehan of Home Rental Services in Overland Park, Kansas, "grabbed a hold of." Her business needs to pull such a specific market that mass-mailing paper of any type is usually a total waste of time.

> Some prospects are next to impossible to reach with traditional mailings. So, sometimes you need to up the ante and make a real statement. A lumpy mail package screams, "Notice me! Open me!"

She finds that putting something lumpy in the mailing at least gets the recipient to open the piece. Now she takes this one step farther. Once a month, she prints colorful flyers, glues individual Hershey kisses to each one and delivers them to the offices of prospective customers. She states, "It is rare that someone turns us away when offering this tiny gift. People started to remember us and watch for their 'kiss.' We even have customers walk into our office with the flyer in their hand—minus the kiss of course" (www.home4rent.com).

How to Run a Lumpy Mail Campaign

To create an effective lumpy mail campaign, start with your core marketing messages, core point of difference, or benefit. These are the primary things you promote when you want to tell your prospects why they should hire you, and these are the elements that you can use to create an effective lumpy mail package.

Now think of some unique items, trinkets, or packaging that you can use to help communicate your Core Message. "We'll jump through hoops to get your business"—the hula hoop. "We're the key to your success"—a box of keys. "We provide total solutions"—a box of Total brand cereal. "We've got the tools to help you get the job done"—a box of play tools. It's important that you create a strong image and metaphor for the message you are trying to communicate.

Repetition

Like any good direct mail campaign, repetition will improve your results. I usually suggest looking at three installments in your campaign. If done correctly, this will usually leave the recipient eager to perform whatever call to action you request at the end of the campaign.

144

A Building Series

A very powerful way to construct your campaign, particularly if your audience is not too familiar with you, is to create your three pieces in a story fashion. Each piece should build on the last and deliver an integrated message. You can use this method to build intrigue. Many times I will send the first piece in a lumpy campaign without a company name, logo, or return address. In each piece, I will imply that there is more to come. The impact of this technique can be strong. In some cases your prospects will actually look forward to getting the next piece. People love a good mystery.

The Call to Action

Like any direct mail advertising campaign, it is important to determine what you want the final outcome or call to action to be and deliver it in the last piece. If you want the recipient to call your office, take your call, visit a Web site, or attend a workshop, make it painfully clear what the point of the game has been.

I've actually had clients tell me that prospects who wouldn't even return their phone calls eagerly made appointments and sometimes still displayed in their office the items they were sent throughout the campaign. I think people don't get this kind of attention much in their lives—and they want it.

How Much for Those Lumps?

It is true that a lumpy mail campaign can get relatively expensive when compared to, say, a postcard mailing, so it's important for you to consider two things when you are designing yours: How many clients do you need, and what is the lifetime value a new client has to your business? In other words, if you can determine that a new client is worth $10,000 annually to your business, then you can more effectively justify spending a certain amount to acquire a new client.

Most small businesses only need a handful of new clients at any given time to thrive. Lumpy mail is perfect for that kind of growth. Carefully target ten new businesses at a time, throw the kitchen sink at them, and watch your appointment rate soar to about 70 percent.

A Consistent Contact Strategy

You've worked on your Duct Tape Marketing System diligently to this point, and you know your prospects need what you sell. You know they want what you sell. Heck, you know that they even sent away for your free information report. But, even with all of that, you are still missing one major piece of the puzzle. No matter what else you know, you may not know the precise point in time when your prospects finally decide to make a purchase of the kind of product or service you have to offer. People search for information and solutions in many different ways and on many different timetables.

Some will buy immediately; some may take a year or more depending on the complexity of the purchase. One of the keys to solving this dilemma is consistent and repeated contact. You must build a marketing system that guarantees your prospects (particularly your "A" prospects that have responded to your two-step ads) are contacted at least eight to ten times a year. This single strategy alone can significantly increase the odds that your name will jump to the top of the list when they actually do decide to purchase.

Dropping useful information, month after month, to your prospects and customers is one of the best trust-building strategies you can employ.

Contact Management Software to the Rescue

David Norcross of 1 Source Graphics, located in Southwest Virginia, feels that contact management software is key to his consistent marketing efforts. First, he determines the types of businesses and industries that would probably purchase his products. He gets this information through the Internet, chamber of commerce guides, or the Yellow Pages. He then plugs these organizations into his contact management software.

Next, he calls the receptionist of that organization, gets the name of the person who can make a purchasing decision for his product, and sends that person a letter. He does not ask to speak to him or her at this time. He follows up the letter in one week with a phone call and works to set an appointment.

He finds that this steady approach allows him to set one appointment for every five letters. He sends five of these letters every working day, which means he makes five follow-up phone calls every day. Therefore, he typically generates one appointment with a new client every day.

If for some reason this person does not want to see him, he puts them on his mailing list to receive a custom activity series set up within his contact management software. Every ten days he sends out a targeted postcard to that person detailing a unique service he provides or giving more information about his work for other clients. After four to six postcards go out to that prospect, he follows up with another call. Frequently though, he receives calls from his postcard mailings. Why? Because they are targeted.

He also uses his mailing to point the potential client to his Web site where he has developed an e-mail autoresponder series that provides additional information to his prospects (www.osprint.net).

A Consistent Pattern of Contact

So, what will you send to your prospects and customers on a monthly basis? Here is an example calendar of contact points:

Month #1—Letter announcing a new service (change to existing service)

Month #2—Newsletter highlighting tips and company news

Month #3—Phone call to discover opportunities

Month #4—Reprint of an industry magazine article of interest

Month #5—Case study of a successful client solution you provided

Month #6—Request for critique of a proposed sales letter (you won't believe how valuable this can be)

Month #7—Time for another newsletter

Month #8—Reprint of an article you contributed to an industry magazine

Month #9—Announce a new service

Month #10—Invite them to a workshop

Month #11—Phone call to introduce someone in your referral network

Month #12—Checklist of helpful tips for your industry/service

Notice that this schedule includes a couple of phone contacts. This can be a very powerful research tool as well as a business-building tool. Sometimes you will learn what your prospects really want and how valuable the materials you are sending them really are to them.

You may want to consider breaking your prospect list into groups based on potential opportunity. Your twenty or thirty "A" prospects might get a copy of your favorite book or some home-made cookies in a tin with your company logo. And if you really want to make a hit with your "A" prospects, take the time to find out some background on them and personalize your marketing materials. If Ed Jones over there at Acme Industries went to Notre Dame (not such a hard thing to find out), you will score major points by simply sending a clipping from some magazine about his favorite subject—the Fighting Irish.

You can even set up Web-based news searches through Google and Yahoo alerts that will find automatically and send you everything that is being said about a school, industry, company, sports team, you name it. So an industry guru makes a prediction for the future of your prospect's industry, and you drop the article in the mail to him. Now who do you think he is going to remember come order time?

Use your contact database of Ideal Prospects, set-up a schedule of different types of contact points like the one above, and then stick to it. And don't forget to include your current clients in that list. Reselling them can lead to more and more business and referrals.

Reactivate the Long Lost Customer

Okay, one last thing. Now that you have your sales letter written and your advertising campaign mapped out, why not go out there and reactivate some lost customers. Any business that has been around for a while has seen clients come and go. Many times clients leave for no other reason than you simply stopped paying attention to them.

Now that you have completely revamped your marketing message and approach, you may have something to entice past customers to come back. A simple way to do this is to tailor your Sticky Sales Letter to send to clients who you no longer do business with and make them an offer to come back and learn about the new and improved you.

Write a headline that lets them know you want to do whatever it takes to get them to come back. You might even consider apologizing to them for your obvious lack of attention, and then make them an offer that helps them get reacquainted.

Some businesses have found this little tool to be very effective in reactivating past clients and immediately creating an upturn in sales.

Duct Tape Marketing Chapter Resources

ACT - CRM and customer database software
www.ducttapemarketing.com/act.php

SageCRM - Online CRM and customer database service
www.ducttapemarketing.com/sagecrm.php

Action Steps

1. Start a swipe file—study and collect successful direct mail letters.
2. Research sources for your perfect direct mail list.
3. Craft your primary sales offer.

Chapter Ten
Earned Media Attention and Expert Status

Defining Public Relations for the Small Business

In 1983 Paul Hartunian (www.paulhartunian.com) became an overnight celebrity when he captured national media attention as the guy who sold the Brooklyn Bridge. All he really did was cart off some construction debris from a crew that was redecking the Brooklyn Bridge and then produce certificates with pieces of the actual bridge. He sent out a little press release with the headline: "Man sells Brooklyn Bridge for $14.95."

Paul's little publicity stunt landed him on the *Phil Donahue Show*, the *Jenny Jones Show*, *To Tell the Truth*, the *Regis Philbin Show*, Johnny Carson's *Tonight Show*, *Smart Money*, *CNN News*, *Forbes*, *Changing Times*, *Redbook*, *New Jersey Monthly*, *Money* magazine, *USA Today*, the *Wall Street Journal*, the *New York Times*, and over one thousand other radio and TV talk shows.

He has since created a multimillion dollar business teaching others how to profit from PR. While a lot has changed in the media since 1983, the principles that drive the effective use of PR as a lead generation tool have not.

So let's start this PR journey with a textbook kind of definition just so we are all on the same page. According to the Duct Tape Marketing system, *public relations activity for the small business consists primarily of gaining positive mention of your company or your products in newspapers, magazines, news shows, newsletters, Web sites, and journals read by some portion of your target market.* There are other activities that fall under the heading of public relations, but for our purposes, this is the definition we will use. PR is also a primary plank of your overall lead generation foundation.

Press coverage can come in the form of a feature story, news brief, announcement, or even a quote in an industry-related story. Many people refer to this as free media, but I like to refer to it as earned media because it does take some systematic effort to make it happen.

In this chapter, I will cover some of the strategies and tools employed by professional public relations firms to help you gain positive press and avoid the pitfalls that cause most business owners to fail in this arena. Obtaining media coverage for your firm is not necessarily difficult, but there are some strategies and tactics that you must understand in order to achieve the greatest success.

Why PR Is so Powerful

Used in conjunction with the other marketing tools presented in the Duct Tape system, PR can help you produce some very impressive lead generation results. Successful placement of a feature story about your firm may produce more actual customers and business than an entire year of Yellow Pages advertising.

Before I spend time trying to educate you on how to generate media coverage for your business, I want to make sure you fully appreciate why it is so important for you to put in the effort to make it happen.

More Credible

People have grown tired of what they see as advertising and consequently tune a great deal of it out. When someone reads about a great new service in a newspaper, they are much more likely to believe that a story is true since the story was written by an objective third party, the reporter.

Great Return

A full-page ad in a magazine that your target market might read can cost thousands of dollars. A story in that same publication might not cost anything at all. But please don't think that you can simply fire off a press release and wait for the phone to ring.

Great Brand Building

A story about your firm or your people or some way in which your firm overcame adversity can help your target market connect with your firm in a much more personal way than any form of advertising or promotion can. This can be a very positive way to help the world understand how your firm is different.

Resells Your Clients

One of the surest ways to grow your business is to do more and more business with existing clients. A favorable story about your firm can help reconvince your current clients that they made the right decision to hire you after all. This can go a long way toward the amount of business you do with them in the future. Never underestimate the power of someone seeing a story and realizing that she discovered you first! This is the kind of recognition that generates word-of-mouth testimonials.

Resells Your Staff

There is a similar impact on workplace pride, which is one of the most important aspects of employee satisfaction. Generating positive press coverage for your organization and your people makes them proud to be a part of your team.

Automatic Marketing Content

In many cases you can reprint articles that appear in newspapers, magazines, and newsletters and use them as additional marketing pieces. While an industry newsletter may not be read by your potential target market, prospects may be impressed when you send them a copy of an article about your firm, even if it appeared in *Modern Plumbing*.

The Keys to Positive PR

There are a handful of practices that can help you achieve much greater results with your PR efforts. Keep in mind that getting positive PR is still a marketing activity. The primary difference is that your target market is a set of reporters, producers, and editors.

Target Your Sources

You should look at PR much like the rest of your marketing efforts. Targeting your media sources, down to a specific reporter that covers your market, is an essential practice. You should create a media prospect list much the same way you create a client prospect list. You must begin to think in terms of building relationships with those media prospects and then turning them into loyal media clients.

A financial planner I know makes a point of having coffee with at least one journalist every month. He doesn't pitch a single thing; he simply discusses what's going on in the markets and what rumors he has heard about potential scoop material. Guess who the reporters call when the rumor materializes?

Read the Publication

One of the most important things you can do when you target a specific publication is to read past issues of the publication. This should be obvious, but experience tells me differently. Nothing will turn off a reporter, an editor, or an entire staff at a publication faster than when you send your press release to a publication that does not cover that area. By reading the publications you target, you will also get a feel for the types of stories and angles they cover.

Start Small

Too many business owners make the mistake of going for the big feature story on the first contact with a publication. To me, this is like trying to get prospects to buy thousands of dollars of services because you faxed them a page of copy about your firm. Occasionally, you may indeed have a story so hot that any reporter who reads about it will call . . . but this is the exception.

Build your relationship with a reporter a step at a time. Send announcements or even letters to the editor first. Then begin to forward useful industry data or trends that you pick up from your association journals. Over time, this type of relationship building will make them much more receptive to your story ideas.

Steve Morsa of Match Engine Marketing, in Thousand Oaks, California, has success with a simple PR tactic. Many print magazines, online e-letters, magazines, and blogs are anxious for insightful, well-written letters to the editor, opinions, and feedback. Steve focuses on these needs and is able to pick up some very nice coverage for two of his business divisions.

All such "letter" submissions include his company Web site

address so that readers can easily get more information about his business (www.matchenginemarketing.com).

Be Consistent

Repetition and consistency pay off. Many businesses send out one press release and give up. When you routinely send good information to reporters, you begin to build some recognition as a credible resource for industry information. Even if your story idea doesn't get picked up, you may eventually receive a call asking for more information or for a quote on another story.

Become a Source

One of the quickest ways to gain favor with reporters is to supply them with useful information. Researching stories is a lot of work. If a member or two of the media can come to depend on you as a source, you will find them turning to you for a quote at deadline time. Don't think in terms of getting a story every time you contact a media prospect. Be willing to give first and you will eventually receive. Have you ever noticed how the media seems to quote the same people from your industry over and over again? You can become that person with a little bit of groundwork. It's well worth the investment of your time.

What Makes a Good Story?

Here is a good rule of thumb to follow when searching for a story angle to present to the media. Ask yourself this question: will the readers of this publication think this is interesting, entertaining, informative, or useful? Self-interested, veiled attempts at promoting your business will fall flat. The media does not care about your company's success unless their readers care about it. The media does not care about your new product unless you can help them understand how their readers are longing to know about the problems it solves.

The following is a list of ways that will help you get a reporter's attention. If you can position your potential story ideas using one or more of these ways, you will have a better chance of success.

> Self-interested, veiled attempts at promoting your business will fall flat. The media does not care about your company's success unless their readers care about it.

Have Real News

There is nothing that gets the media's attention like news. Now, what you think is news may not actually be newsworthy, but if you have won a significant contract or licensed a new technology, you may indeed have a story that provides a reporter with a news angle.

Be First

Everyone seems fascinated with things that are first: the first company to feature a technology, the first company to do a certain type of project, the first company in the area to win a national award. Of course there are ways to be a new kind of first: the first woman- or minority-owned business in your industry to do something of note is also a first.

Be Unique

Sometimes you can receive positive publicity simply by doing or offering something that is unique. An unheard of guarantee, service technicians in tuxedos, or balloon telegrams for marketing are all examples of unique practices.

Local Angles on National Stories

If some aspect of your business is making national headlines, you may be able to weigh in with the local press on a local angle of the story. Local news reporters often prefer to quote local sources even when they are covering a national story. Has some legislation recently passed that impacts your industry? Has a major lawsuit been settled? Is a new product, service, or innovation receiving coverage? It is critical that you watch the national news trends to stay on top of these opportunities.

Ties to a Trend

Your association and industry publications often report on industry and marketing trends. Reporters love to get a jump on a coming trend. You can put yourself in the middle of a story by simply pointing out something that may be happening in other parts of the country that ties your company or product to a recognized trend.

Overcoming Adversity

Everyone loves a story with a great ending. If you or your firm has overcome some adversity, this may be a great source for a story.

People Stories

Promotions, new hires, awards, board appointments, weddings, births, and all other manner of events that involve people in your firm and what they do on and off the job can be a good source for story ideas. Maybe your company's softball team hasn't won or lost a game in ten years. Maybe your firm has repaired eight houses for a charitable organization this year. Perhaps your firm has a college tuition reimbursement program that is far better than most, and you have four new college graduates at the firm to prove it.

Solving a Common Problem

If you have discovered a unique way to solve a problem your target market has or that impacts other firms in your same industry, you may have a story idea. Business publications in particular are always on the lookout for innovative business practices. Don't just think in terms of some solution to a client need. Maybe you've discovered a successful way to attract prospective employees. These stories will often be read by potential clients and really help tell how your firm is different. In addition, it is easy to show how these types of stories can benefit the readership of a publication without appearing too self-serving.

Contrary to Popular Belief

A little understood PR approach that has worked wonders over the years is to sit back, view the current landscape, and then find a way to present a marketing argument that goes against a current fad or perception.

This strategy can be a great way to win occasional media attention. Media folks are commonly taught to get both sides of the story. So, if everyone is preaching the merits of X, they will search high and low for someone who says Y.

The point is, you should look around your industry for ways to buck trends or start trends and then publish an article, letter to the editor, blog post, or ad to help differentiate your way of thinking. Be careful, though; contrariness for contrariness' sake or bucking a belief that is so firmly established as to be beyond a trend can end up making you look foolish.

Minor Story Topic Starters

Use the following questions to help you brainstorm for potential PR topics. One of the surest ways to get *more* media coverage is to get *some* media coverage. Start small but be consistent. It is a good practice to attempt to get some form of coverage every month. The more successful you are in terms of sheer volume of coverage the easier it is to get full-length feature coverage. Is that Oprah on the phone?

- Have there been any personnel changes, promotions, or additions in your firm?
- Have you taken on a new partner?
- Are you planning to expand your operations?
- Have you landed a significant new project or customer?
- Are you conducting educational seminars?
- Have employees completed industry apprenticeships or certifications?
- Are you planning to speak at a professional organization's meeting?
- Have you, or anyone on your staff, received an award in your industry?
- Has a trade association cited you for excellence?
- Have you, or any of your staff, been elected to serve on the board of directors for another company or volunteer organization?
- Has your company sponsored a charitable fund-raising event in the community?
- Are you doing anything that is a new trend in your industry?
- Are you mentoring other business owners or students?

- Does your business have a high number of women or minorities in management positions?
- Have you supported one or more of your employees through unusual crises?
- Do you offer any unusual employee benefits or incentives?
- Have you solved a problem in your industry?
- Is your marketing unique?
- Have you started a new department or business?
- Have you significantly expanded your current services?
- Have you moved to new or larger offices or substantially renovated your offices?
- Have you become a new dealer for a name brand product?
- Has your company been in business for 5, 10, 15, 25, or 50 years?
- Have your discovered new ways to use technology in your business?
- Have you discovered new ways to market your products or services?
- Have you increased your sales since last year? Is that unusual for your industry in today's economy?
- What's the income trend in your industry? Are you following the trend or breaking out of the mold?
- Do you have a strong opinion on a local situation or community problem? Can you offer a solution? For example, a construction company might devise a way to organize leftover construction job site materials to benefit an organization that repairs homes for low-income residents.

The Story Beyond the Story

If possible you should always try to plan stories that may create other stories. In other words, look at your story idea as a series of press releases. Let's say that you have donated your firm's services to paint the local senior center. While the donation itself is a wonderful thing to do, you can get the most mileage from a PR standpoint if you do these things: announce the arrangement, announce the painting day activity, and plan a little get together at the center to "reopen" with a fresh coat of paint. (Pictures are great here.) The idea is to keep the presses rolling. In some cases you may actually get two or three follow-up stories, but the main point is to change your thinking about how to create stories in general.

Your Media Prospect List

It is a good idea to create or buy a database of media contacts and store this list in your ACT or other contact database much like your prospect list. With a little bit of research on the Internet, you can most likely compile your own local list of publications and reporters that cover your industry. Most media Web sites feature staff lists. Radio and television stations often feature talk shows and news digest shows that are always hungry for interesting stories. Make sure that you research these opportunities as well. Each program will have a producer that is often responsible for lining up guests.

Don't forget to add media contacts or newsletter publishers for chambers of commerce, trade associations, clubs you are a member of, and even universities you attended. These organizations feel obliged to publish announcements from members and may provide some good coverage for your business.

John Ristow, Communications Manager for the Broward Teachers Union in Ft. Lauderdale, Florida, sends press releases to local media outlets but also includes government agencies, non-profit organizations, and elected leaders in his media list. This allows the message to reach the intended news sources but also keeps key community leaders and constituencies informed of his organization's important activities.

There are also several national companies that sell media lists, such as Bacon's, Gebbie Press, and MediaPost.

What if you don't know where to send your PR materials?

If you don't really know a specific reporter's name at a publication you are trying to interest in your story idea, I suggest that you call whoever you think might cover it and ask this question: If I wanted to submit a story idea about design trends in commercial building (or whatever your particular story idea is) would you be the person I should send it to?

It's funny, but for some reason reporters really respond to this exact question. If they are the source, you've pitched them your story idea without them knowing it, and if they are not your source, they will normally tell you who is. Either way you've made a productive call.

Sending anything off to a publication without a real live name attached to it is probably a waste of time. Do your research and find out the right name. It is a good idea to verify your media contacts as reporters change beats and publications often.

The PR Toolbox—Creating Sticky Pitch Letters, Press Releases, and PR Kits

The primary publicity tools in the Duct Tape Marketing PR system are the pitch letter, the press release, and the publicity kit. Below you will find specific information about how to create and format each to put them to work for your business. Later on in this chapter I will show you how to use each of the tools systematically to earn media attention.

The Pitch Letter

A pitch letter is a very effective way to interest a reporter in your story idea or present your specific expertise as a perfect guest for a show. The pitch letter is a bit like an ad for your story idea. It is typically written much like a short letter and sells your story to the reader. Later in this chapter, I introduce the press release and a way to use the pitch letter with a press release, but at this point it is important that you understand that a pitch letter is not a press release. A pitch letter should simply set the table for your idea, not present the specific details of your idea. Ideally, the reader of a pitch letter should be led to think, *This sounds like something I should find out more about.* Here are some ways to write powerful pitch letter:

- *Don't waste a word*: Hit journalists with your best shot right off the bat. In the first sentence, give them the angle for your story idea that makes it worth their attention.
- *Customize it*: It is very important that you tailor your pitch to the people who will receive it. Let them know that you understand that your story could fit their readers. In fact, you may want to emphasize specific aspects of your story pitch that would be most appropriate for their publication. If you know that the readers of a certain publication are seniors, then point out why your pitch is of particular interest to seniors.
- *Prove that it fits their readership*: The first question that an editor or reporter is programmed to ask themselves when they encounter a story pitch is, "Why would our reader care about this story?" Your pitch should complete this statement: "This story would make a valuable addition to your coverage on the recent trend of . . ."

Obviously, the more you do your homework on a specific publication, the easier it will be to write powerful pitch letters. Here's just one example:

Blogging as new business marketing tool is hot.

Plenty has been written about what a blog is and even about the fact that blogging is a powerful marketing tool. The story that no one is telling yet, though, is what results these businesses are experiencing—if any—by using a blog.

I started the Duct Tape Marketing blog (http://www.ducttapemarketing.com/weblog.php) about 2 1/2 years ago because I thought the technology sounded like a perfect way to spread my marketing message. And now I can point to some very measurable returns on my blogging investment.

For example: Very soon after launching my blog it became apparent that this was not only a great publishing tool but also a great way to build a loyal group of readers and to network with other like-minded online folks. (Seth Godin told me that he loves my blog.)

Not long after that, as the blog as a business tool trend started picking up steam, I received requests to do interviews on business blogging for *Costco Connection*, *Entrepreneur*, *Inc.*, *CiscoIQ*, and the *Washington Post*.

Several large online publishers such as the Marketing Sherpa and About.com started calling my blog the "best small business marketing blog" and "one of the top 10 most practical small business blogs."

This summer, *Forbes* named my blog a *Forbes* favorite for both the small business and marketing categories in their "Best of the Web issue."

I think the readers of your publication would benefit from

a story about the business benefits of blogging, and I can help you tell this story from experience.

I will contact you to discuss.

Regards,
John Jantsch

The Press Release

The press release is still the workhorse of your PR program, but in order to have success with it you must follow certain guidelines. Keep in mind that you cannot simply write a press release and send it off to the media and expect coverage. The press release is just a piece of your entire PR system, but very little will happen until you understand how to craft an effective press release.

Media outlets will rarely use the content in your press release for a story, but you can bet they will dismiss your pitch for a story if they feel you don't understand how to write a press release.

One Page—One Subject

The point of a press release is to get the attention of a reporter and editor and make them want to know more about your story or firm. Many people believe that writing a press release is like handing a reporter a story. This single assumption will ruin your PR efforts. There are some isolated cases in which a publication may use the facts in your press release or announcement to fill some space, but we repeat for emphasis: the purpose of a press release is to get attention so you can talk to a reporter who wants to know more. That's it.

Keep your press release to one page and focus on one topic. Some reporters get hundreds of story ideas every day. If your press release is three or four pages long, chances are they won't even look at it. Get their attention, then offer up a story when they call. In fact, if you can leave them hanging and wondering just a bit, all the better.

How to Format a Press Release

If you understand that the purpose of a press release is to grab attention, then you might also begin to realize that there is a bit of an art to writing an effective one.

This art actually begins with proper format. It probably shouldn't matter how you format a good story, but editor after editor has told me that if a press release comes to them and is not properly formatted, it often doesn't get read. Read that again if you are bit of a maverick. If you want to read about your company in the news, then you might just have to follow the rules. Ultimately your story will have to stand on its own, but follow this accepted format. You stand a better chance of making that all-important first impression.

For release. The very first thing to appear on your release is the release date or time. If your story is for immediate release, say so: "For Immediate Release." If there is a reason to hold some news or a seasonal deadline, say so: "For Release before Halloween." Some background-type releases can also carry the "Release at Will" tag.

Contact information. Don't make it hard for them to get in touch with you. Right under the release info, state your name, address, direct phone, and e-mail address under the heading "For more information." Remember the real point is to get them to call you.

The headline. You've already learned that up to 90 percent of all advertising effectiveness rides on the effectiveness of the headline. It is no different for a press release. Most readers and reporters will decide whether or not you have anything to say based solely on the grabbing power of your headline. Pull them in quickly. Write five or six attention grabbing headlines, and then put your release away for day or so. Come back and see which ones still grab you. It is that important.

Typical Headline:
> *ABC Construction Wins Award for Project*

Attention-grabbing headline:
> *Local Contractor Outguns the Big Boys, Steals Coveted Prize*

Dateline. At the start of the body of your release, you are expected to provide some useful information. First give the date of the release and then the city the release originates from. Put a dash after the city and then start the body of your release: "February 18, 2003—Kansas City, MO—Today in history . . . "

Double-space. Double-space the body of your release. This probably goes back to the days when reporters made notes by pencil in the space between the lines, but I guess some still do that.

First paragraph. Okay, so now your headline grabbed them. Tell them what you're going to tell them in the first paragraph. Don't beat around the bush or try to be cute here. Hit them with your best shot.

Quotes and credentials. Quotes make for interesting reading. Try to find a newspaper story without a quoted source of some sort. Add your own quotes and then add some credentials to the person you attribute the quote to. If it's you and you're a master plumber with twenty-five years of experience, then say so. "'The flora and fauna was breathtaking,' said Bill Sphenkle, one of Kansas City's most experienced plumbers."

Call to action. If you want them to interview you or visit your Web site to find out more information, then say so. "Bill Sphenkle is available for interviews." Just don't hype your company or product. Nothing gets your release tossed faster.

Boilerplate. A boilerplate on a press release is a concise paragraph that sums up your company. It is placed at the end of every press release. It is an old newspaper term for a block of copy that is used over and over again.

ABC Construction is located in Upper East Yorktown and was founded in 1967. The company specializes in new pavement construction and maintenance. For more information visit www.ABC-Construction.com.

End. At the end, add the symbol # # #.

Here is an example of a press release:

For Immediate Release
Contact: Ted Williams
SpectraGraphics
TedW@SpectraGraphics.com
800-728-6828

"How to Slash Your Costs on Really Cold Labels"
10 little-known money-saving tips for thermal labeling

Lenexa, KS—SpectraGraphics Label Systems has released a quarter century of labeling knowledge in a free white paper titled—How to Slash Your Thermal Labeling Costs. The 8-page paper is a compilation of 10 little-known tips for those who need labels to function in hot, cold and damp conditions.

The content for the guide was developed from real-life labeling issues and challenges and focuses on ways to cut label costs and reduce label waste.

"Anyone who prints, applies, or buys thermal labels should read this guide," said Ted Williams, president of SpectraGraphics.

Interested parties can obtain a free downloadable copy of the guide online at http://www.spectragraphics.com/ThermalLabels.htm or by calling 800-728-6828.

SpectraGraphics has been designing, engineering, and printing labels specifically for every imaginable use on plastic and plastic containers for over 25 years.

Your Publicity Kit

Your PR program will benefit from the careful creation of a publicity kit. This is essentially a fancy term for a pocket folder filled with a collection of press releases and relevant photos. If you have read the information contained in the marketing kit chapter, you are well on your way to understanding what you need for a press kit. Much of the information is similar to your marketing materials, only formatted and presented in a slightly different manner.

After you complete these documents you should assemble a handful of kits and have them on hand. If you are presenting a specific topic or press release, you can always add it as needed. It is a good idea to send the entire press kit to reporters even if they only request one piece of information. You never know what might get their attention.

The following is a list of some of the essential press releases that your publicity kit should contain.

Backgrounder. This release should give the reader a full accounting of the history and background of the firm, including the types of clients you work with and projects you typically complete.

Your core message. The Core Message release should highlight the primary benefits of doing business with your firm. This is where you can promote the ways your firm is different. When writing a press release, keep in mind that it cannot read like an ad for your firm. Stick to facts and stay away from hype. Think of this release as a document that announces how your firm is different.

Service descriptions. Describe the services that your firm specializes in.

Process descriptions. Describe any unique processes that your firm has implemented. If you have a 24-point daily job site clean-up routine, then explain it.

Case studies. Outline the specifics of some recently completed projects. Again, don't sell, just explain the type of job, any challenges you may have encountered, and the overall result of the project. If you work with several distinct markets you may consider one for each market.

Founders. Include a page or so on each of the firm's owners or partners. Tell about industry background and experience.

A word about photos. Each founder of the firm should have a recent 5" x 7" black and white print or high-quality digital photo on hand at all times. In your press kit, you should include a photo of each as well as some representative product photos. If you have a digital camera and can take photos that are professional in nature, and at least 300 dpi, then do so. If not, it may be wise to hire a photographer or visit a studio to have professional photos taken.

The Duct Tape Marketing Pitch and Release Program

Now that you have a better understanding of the essential PR tools and how to create them in an effective, sticky way, it is time to turn your attention to the art of contacting media outlets. There are essentially four ways that you go about planting PR seeds with the media. Your Duct Tape Marketing PR system will make use of all four in some combination. The decision to use one strategy over another will depend largely on how much interest you can generate for a particular story idea and the particular journalist you are approaching.

The Release as Bait

In certain cases, you may simply write a powerful release for one of your minor themes and send it out or publish it to a press release distribution service such as PRWeb. This approach will rarely net a feature story, but it may attract the attention of a local publication and can also provide links back to your Web site as content publishers syndicate news feeds. This approach should be reserved for announcement-type releases and not for feature-type stories.

The Telephone Pitch

Some journalists like the quick phone pitch. If you are doing your work and building relationships with your targeted reporters, then this approach can be very effective. You simply call the journalist and say, "I have a story idea that I think your reader would like to hear" and then quickly pitch the idea and why the idea makes sense.

In some cases you will get a polite dismissal, but I've often found that a reporter will give you a suggestion or ask a question that will allow you to transform your pitch idea on the fly. This may take some practice, but it's a great way to create stories with a journalist in mind and get coverage.

The Pitch and Release

If you are trying to develop a feature-type story, you will want to put on a full-blown marketing campaign. This is best done by crafting a very compelling pitch letter and powerful press release and sending both to a targeted journalist.

A word of caution on feature stories: try to target one reporter at a time. Take your best shot with that reporter and only move on to the next when it is clear that the publication has no interest in your story. Unless you have really big, breaking news, you need to pitch your story like an exclusive engagement. In some cases, you can even tell the reporter that you want to give them the idea first. Many local publications compete for content, and you can hurt your PR status if your story hits Paper Number One on Tuesday and Paper Number Two on Wednesday. Also, be careful not to pitch several reporters within the same publication. This can get you blacklisted.

Follow Up

After you send a reporter a story pitch or press release, it is a very good idea to follow up by telephone. Sometimes you just need to verify that your release made it to the intended party, but often your follow-up can get your story idea a little more consideration. The key to good follow-up is that when you call, you must be able to offer more information. I like to state that I have some new information with regard to the release I sent.

Reporters are very busy and can become irritated if you simply call and ask if they received your press release. When you call and add some detail or fact to your story, your call will be better received. In fact, some PR pros like to hold on to a critical fact or piece of information in hopes that the journalist is enticed enough to want the missing piece.

The Media Interview

So, what happens when all of your PR activity actually prompts a reporter to call for an interview? Getting the interview is only one half of the deal. Follow the steps below and you are more likely to turn your interview into a powerful marketing tool.

Set Goals for the Interview

When a reporter calls to schedule an interview, either by phone or in person, ask a couple of innocent questions. Find out the nature of the story he is working on, who the audience is, and when he expects it to run. The answers to these questions will help you better prepare your responses.

Never Wing It

The primary point of almost any interview you will be asked to give is to get your company's Core Message communicated in a compelling manor. To do this in the context of an interview, you should script very quotable Core Message sound bites, no more than twenty seconds or so in length, and be prepared to deliver them word for word at the appropriate time.

Break the Ice

When a reporter that you may not know calls to interview you, there is often a bit of a control issue. The reporter is asking all the questions, so she is in control. You actually want to wrestle some of this away right up front. Think about this like you would a sales call. In order for you to get your message told, you may need to interject it into the discussion.

I find that asking a couple of ice-breaking questions can be a great way to settle your nerves and open up the reporter. My favorite questions are to ask reporters where they are from or what brought them to this specific publication. Establishing a little personal ground seems to make everyone a little more relaxed.

Redirect

Sometimes reporters just won't get what you are trying to communicate. Or worse, they seem to want to talk about everything but the key points you are trying to communicate. It's not that they are intentionally being difficult; most of the time it is because they may not really know much about your industry. In these cases you need to have a few redirecting phrases that allow you to answer their questions with your answers. Here are several that work wonders:

- What's important to consider in this case, though . . .
- Let me make that more relevant for your readers . . .
- What we can take from that point is . . .
- That's a good example, but I think you'd also be interested in knowing . . .

The key to redirecting a question from a journalist, of course, is to have a plan and preset answers. Then all you have to do is be alert for the proper way to direct the journalist to your message.

Don't Panic

Sometimes you will get a question that you don't have an answer for. Don't panic and don't make up an answer. Simply tell the journalist that you don't know the answer, but promise to get it. This can give you a great excuse to follow up with a reporter. Oftentimes, you remember some other points you wish you had made, and you can add them during a follow-up call.

One Last Thing

I find that it's good to get the last word. Many journalists have been schooled to finish an interview with an open-ended question like, "Is there anything else you'd like our readers to know about . . ." This a great sound bite opportunity, and you should always have a prepared comment that is very powerful. Even if the reporter doesn't ask, I like to interject this last statement, "You know, there's one more thing I'd like to point out . . ."

Prepare a Takeaway

Make it as easy as you can for the journalist to get the facts and figures right. Prepare some sort of takeaway that will help your story and make sure that all of your contact information and you're your Web sites and other places to find more information are included.

Ways to Extend Your Media Attention

Once you get your PR system up and running, you should look for ways to integrate it into all of your marketing efforts. When you receive any media coverage, make sure that you reprint the article and format it in a way that you can use it in your marketing kit or as part of a mailing sent to your clients and prospects.

How to Get More out of Your Press Releases

Print several hundred copies of the release—in the press release format described below—and send it to your clients and hottest prospects. When you do this little bit of direct mail PR for a while, your clients and prospects will start to mention that they keep seeing you in the press somewhere and things must be going great.

What I've discovered is that with the blur of information coming to us everyday, people can no longer keep track of what they saw where. Over time, your press releases will become media coverage to your readers. This practice may sound odd, but I know from experience it works.

Think Nationally

Don't forget national sources even if your business is local. Nothing will make your company more attractive to the local media, potential clients, and even lenders than a story about your firm in a national publication. There are many resources to help you locate national press contacts and national press release distribution services. If you have a unique enough angle, it may be well worth investing in national attention.

Writing Articles for Publicity

Many publications, newsletters, and online e-zines accept articles contributed by experts in their field. You are an expert at what you do, so writing and submitting articles to publications read by your target market is a powerful way to build your reputation as an expert. When you write an article about a topic relevant to your target market, you can greatly enhance your appeal to that market.

Building an entire library of articles is also a powerful way to supplement your marketing kit, educational program, or Web site content. There are many online article directories that would be happy to accept your articles in exchange for a link back to your Web site.

Published articles also provide you with a very credible tool for your referral sources to share with the people they may send your way. Again, the article is seen as much more credible because it appears in a publication as opposed to your sales materials.

Look for publications that may have an interest in allowing you to contribute on a regular basis. Small publications are often understaffed and very eager to accept well-written articles.

Marilyn O'Hearne of Connections Coaching in Shawnee Mission, Kansas, works with clients who want to make changes; this sometimes involves a career change, so she reads the *Kansas City Star* (her local newspaper) career section. Several years ago, they were rotating national career columns. When she inquired about contributing, they asked for and liked her writing sample. The newspaper ended up rotating her column with the national ones, appreciating the local connection. She actually got paid for getting her name and business "out there."

From there, she contacted a local magazine's online editor about another column. After displaying her previous columns, she was able to negotiate an even more lucrative contract with the online magazine (www.marilynoh.com).

Steven Van Yoder of Get The Word Out Communications and author of *Get Slightly Famous* claims that the most effective tactic he has found is to write one magazine article a month. He then uses a multi-prong strategy to get it published in a variety of media that reach his target market. This includes local newspapers, magazines, trade journals, and Web sites that reach his prospects. He uses the reprints as effective, low-cost marketing materials.

Using this strategy has allowed him to make a major impact in his marketing, on an ongoing basis, in as little as a half a day a month. This approach allows him to leverage one piece of writing in several ways (www.getslightlyfamous.com).

Action Steps

1. Target your media sources, including a growing list of Internet-based media and news resources.
2. Create three or four central media themes for the year that support your core marketing message.
3. Create a list of ten to twelve minor, but interesting, marketing-related themes for ongoing PR.
4. Create a PR calendar, and assign a PR theme and goal for each month.
5. Write a fully developed pitch for each of your major themes.

6. Formulate one-page press releases with catchy headlines for each of your minor themes.
7. Once a month, target your core media list and distribute a press release or pitch for a major theme.
8. Follow up with your core media list by telephone and offer some new piece of news or trend angle that you did not include in your pitch or press release.
9. Track media coverage in local and trade press, set-up Google Alerts for a number of key related terms and reprint for marketing purposes any media coverage received.
10. Send handwritten thank you notes (or T-shirts) to members of the media to thank them for an interview or mention.

Chapter Eleven
Ramp Up a Systematic
Referral Machine

O ur lead generation system is coming along nicely, but without
a fully functioning referral marketing system, we're missing
the important third leg of a lead generation machine. When we
combine a referral marketing system with the advertising and PR
systems presented previously, your lead generation machine will
be a fully operational, very firm, and powerful foundation.

What Is Referral Marketing?

Simply put, referral marketing is a specific set of strategies and
tools designed to bring the small business owner new clients,
qualified leads, and repeat business without the aid of, or in addition to, other advertising methods.

Many business owners have built thriving businesses entirely
upon referrals. Almost all businesses get started this way. The
business lands a client, does some good work, and that client tells
his or her family and friends. Before you know it, this kind of
word-of-mouth marketing creates a steady stream of projects. The
sad thing, though, is that many of these same businesses never
realize they could generate even more business if they actively par-
ticipated in the generation of referrals.

Some professionals, such as lawyers, doctors, and accountants, are particularly suited to referral marketing. Very few people feel comfortable hiring a doctor based on that doctor's ad in the Yellow Pages. When looking for a professional of this nature, most ask someone they trust for a referral.

As a rule of thumb, the more personal or the more expensive a service is, the more likely it is that a potential client will seek the advice of another. A window washing company, for example, whose crew may spend a great deal of time going from room to room in a client's house, will benefit greatly from referrals.

Why Referral Marketing Is so Powerful

Experience tells me that there are two things that often hold small business owners back from taking full advantage of referral marketing: the lack of a system and the presence of fear.

Most of this chapter is about building a referral marketing system, so I want to spend some time up front helping you get over the fear of making referrals a core part of your marketing.

When I say fear, I mean things like fear of being rejected, fear that you will appear to be begging for business, or fear that your existing clients don't really care about helping you build your business.

> There are two things that often hold small business owners back from taking full advantage of referral marketing: the lack of a system and the presence of fear.

All I can say to you this is—get over it. If you provide a product or service that helps people solve problems and meet needs, then you are doing a disservice to your customers and the world in general if you don't actively seek referrals. I don't think I could say it much more passionately than that.

If you think that your clients will be put off by your desire to involve them in helping you grow your business, you aren't thinking about the relationship the way you should. The entire act of generating a referral comes down to two simple things:

1. Providing a product or service that people like
2. Managing the referral expectation

With a Duct Tape Marketing systematic approach to generating referrals, part two of that equation is done, but let me give you some more reasons why you should bring referral marketing to the top of your marketing thinking.

People Love to Give Referrals

If you have any resistance to asking for referrals, you need to know that people just love to give referrals. They like to feel that maybe they helped another person grow his or her business. It feels good.

People also like to demonstrate how smart they are. When clients find a business that provides a solution, makes their life better, or just plain saves them money, they like to talk about it. They like to tell anyone who will listen that they got a great deal. So don't hold back—ask for referrals. You're actually doing them a favor.

Great Return on Investment

From a financial sense, referral marketing can get you the best bang for your buck. Depending upon the specific methods you choose, a referral marketing system can be implemented at very little, if any, cost. Done correctly, there will always be some cost involved, but compared to traditional advertising, referral marketing can provide the greatest return on your investment of time and money.

More Qualified Clients

As long as you have developed your ideal target market and communicated who your ideal clients are, then the referrals you receive are likely to be a much better fit than those generated from some advertising campaigns.

Borrowed Credibility and Trust

Potential clients are looking to work with firms they can trust. Frankly, they don't trust your advertising. They expect that you will say great things about your firm or your service. When someone they already trust says you're all right, then you, in effect, borrow that trust.

Fewer Issues Regarding Price

When clients come to you because their best friend said you would be the tops at providing something they needed, they not only expect to pay a premium for your services, they are willing to do so because they attach a higher value to your service due to your relationship with that best friend.

It Makes You Better

If your firm is going to make referral marketing a key marketing strategy, then the primary objective for everyone in your firm will become making every client so happy that they are dying to send their friends, family, and associates your way. If that were everybody's job, including yours, would that change the way you served your clients? Would that have an impact on your business?

I have seen companies change completely by simply adopting this mind-set.

What Motivates Someone to Refer You?

I have studied the idea of referral marketing for years and, when designing a referral marketing system, it almost always comes down to answering this simple question: what would motivate someone to refer you?

The good news is—the answer is always the same: people refer businesses, services, products, people, movies, barbers—you name it—if it makes them look and feel good. The bad news—designing a system that gets at this answer can be tricky.

People want to pass along a smart buy, a new find, a great experience—in part because it makes them look and feel smart, loyal, counted on, savvy, cutting edge, crafty—whatever the reason, they need to look good. I'm not pointing this out as some cynical conclusion about the world—I'm pointing this out to say that any successful referral marketing effort you engage in better give your referral source this motivation.

I guess another way of saying it is that no one wants to refer something or someone that makes them look bad.

Rules of Referral Marketing

There are two key sources to draw upon when looking for referrals. Many business owners find the best sources of referrals are existing clients. Existing clients, after all, know your business and should be one of your best word-of-mouth advertisers.

There are many professions that also count on networks of professionals to supply referrals. Accountants often refer new clients to attorneys, financial planners, and even payroll services. In my experience, it doesn't really matter what business you are in, you should develop referral tactics that allow you to generate referral leads from both your existing clients and a targeted referral network. Often, you will find that the right strategic referral network partners have the ability to generate significantly more referrals than your customers.

While your existing clients can appreciate your work, they may not be as motivated as a strategic partner. In other words, a business that serves your same market and has several hundred existing clients may be highly motivated to refer his entire client base in order to help them get the great service you can provide.

Deserve Referrals

I suppose it goes without saying, but if your current clients are not satisfied with the level of service they receive, then you can bet they will not refer many new clients. Sometimes you must fix your internal business in order to wow clients and turn them into referral machines. Start by asking yourself this simple question: "What could we do that would make our clients so happy they would look for ways to refer new clients?"

Target Your Referral Sources

Just as you must define and target your best customer prospect, you must also have a very specific profile of the best referral sources. In many cases, this is simply the profile of your best customer. The idea is that if your top customers could help you land one or two just like themselves, then your business would exponentially explode.

As I stated previously, in addition to a target list from your client base, you must also develop a target prospect list made up of other professional contacts who have already earned the trust of members of your target market.

Attorneys are often great referral sources for accountants or financial planners, and vice versa. Many painting contractors work with roofers and gutter specialists. The point is that you must target these types of referral sources and create a system that allows you to develop these relationships much like client relationships.

Jason J. Culbertson of The Culbertson Team Real Estate Solutions in Paola, Kansas, gives his top fifty referral prospects an empty, two-inch, three-ring binder. Included with the binder is a letter that states the binder is to be used for the marketing materials he sends to them, including but not limited to newsletters, postcards, letters, and holiday and birthday cards. The letter also states that anyone who keeps everything in this binder, all year long, will be entered into a drawing for a gift certificate to the restaurant of their choice. He personally checks the contents of each binder in December and chooses ten winners.

He hand delivers the binders to save on shipping and gets another one-on-one contact. The ten winners have turned into my raving fans and his best referral sources because they are constantly saving and reading his mailings (www.TheTCTZone.com).

Make It an Expectation

One of the best ways to leverage the power of referral marketing is to make the providing of referrals an expectation of every client relationship. With every new client or networking relationship, you need to introduce the ideas of referrals. In fact, the most effective referral marketing systems start with this as a stated expectation.

This method of generating referrals becomes easier as you implement it. More and more new clients will come to you in this same way and will already understand this expectation.

Do It During the Honeymoon

Your referral marketing system should be designed to acquire referrals as soon as possible. No matter how great your service is, your firm will never be thought of as highly as when you first provide a solution.

Over time, even though you might provide the same great solution over and over again, your value fades with familiarity. Ask for your referrals very early in the relationship.

Educate Your Sources

Much of the work you did at the beginning of this book, describing your Ideal Prospect and carving out your Core Message, will be the foundation for the referral marketing education component of your system. One of the keys to systematically generating high quality referrals is to create a simple tool that helps educate your sources. This tool does not need to be anything complicated or glamorous. One sheet of paper with the following bits of information is more than enough.

What you want. Your referral sources need to know precisely the type of referral you are looking for. (Think of your best customers.)

Your Core Message. Even your best clients may not understand the full range of products or services you are capable of providing. Business owners sometimes complain that they get too many leads that don't match their business when they ask for referrals. A tool to properly educate your referral sources can all but do away with this constraint.

Your referral marketing process. In other words, let your referral sources know how you intend to contact the referral, what you intend to say, and how you intend to follow up. Some referral sources are reluctant to recommend friends and family because they aren't sure what you will do with the referral. The last thing anyone wants is to be known as the person who unleashed the "never say die" salesperson on Uncle Bob.

Remember, when people give you referrals, particularly the

types of referrals described in this publication, they are, in effect, lending you some portion of the trust they have developed with their contact. They may be risking some aspect of their relationship with that referral, so your referral marketing system must make them feel comfortable. The best way to do this is to simply show them your system. This simple step may also help resell them on continuing to work with you.

A call to action. Your referral marketing education tool should end by instructing your source on the best way to refer you. Give them the actual words you would like them to use, the way to turn over a lead, or a Web site address that they should send referral prospects to.

The Perfect Introduction in Reverse

Now that you have developed your education and introduction piece for your referral marketing system, I want to introduce you to one heck of a powerful twist on using this tool. Create a blank form based on your education process, send it out to a list of potential network resources (people who serve the same target market), and ask them to complete it for themselves and send it back to you so you will be better prepared to refer them.

One client got a 65 percent response rate to this very tactic and found referrals coming at him from places he had tried long and hard to penetrate.

Make It Easy for Them

Your referral sources want to give you referrals, but you've got to make it as easy as possible. Everyone is stretched in a hundred different ways. Don't make your referral sources jump through hoops to give you referrals. Make it as easy as possible for them, and you will receive many more referrals.

I've already said that you need to educate them on *whom* to refer, but you may also need to show them *how* to refer. This may mean giving them a script, writing them a recommended referral letter, or even plopping a list of your hottest prospects down in front of them. Create a whole series of referral tools, and put them in the hands of those you know can best refer you to others.

Here are some of my favorite examples:

- Mail a personal letter and enclose a "proposed letter of referral" that simply needs to be copied onto their letterhead.
- Send four referral-type postcards, already stamped and ready for them to send.
- Send them a supply of business cards.
- Give your referral source a supply of pens with your company logo.
- Put a list of prospects in front of them and ask them if they can help you with anyone on your target list.

Be easy to refer and you will be the provider of choice when the referral moment arises.

Follow Up!

It's always a good idea to keep your referral sources involved and motivated. Let them know when you have contacted a referral. Let them know how it went. And, by all means, let them know when one of those referrals turns into a new client.

Your referral sources provide referrals because they want to see your firm prosper. The bigger the role they see themselves playing in that, the more involved they will become. Thank your referral sources in meaningful and genuine ways.

Create Win-Win Motivation

If you've found an effective way to generate business, teach your referral resources how to do it as well. Help them get what they want before you ever ask for a referral, and you will find referrals coming your way in droves.

Kris Gay of Making Memories Photo & Video in Fort Wayne, Indiana, markets her photography services to bakers, caterers, florists, bridal shops, reception sites, nail salons, and beauty shops— all places where her brides are sure to shop.

When she shoots a wedding for a client she also shoots photos of the cake, flowers, dresses, reception room, hair dos, and buffet tables. Then she visits shops with example photos from weddings using that shop's services. She gives the shop a framed enlargements (with her logo and Web site address on them of course) and copies of an information binder that they can use to present her services to potential clients.

The promotion is so successful that she doesn't even bother asking if the store wants the photo. When she shows up with a framed print, they are usually so bowled over that they start looking for somewhere to hang it up right then and there (www. makingmemoriesphoto.com).

Reward Your Sources

There are many ways to provide incentives and rewards to your referral sources. Some industries regulate this very strictly and disallow any form of compensation for referrals, but many do not. You should also note there are many forms of compensation in addition to a straight monetary offer.

You can offer a lower price to clients who refer. You can thank them with gifts. You can reward them with products, or you can simply recognize them at a referral appreciation dinner. You can acknowledge their contribution to your company online and in a newsletter. You can refer business back to them. Use your imagination.

Look for Moments of Truth

There is no perfect time to ask for referrals, but there are some milestones or "moments of truth" events that present perfect opportunities to maximize your ability to receive referrals:

- When you complete a project well done and a client tells you how pleased he or she is
- When you go over and above in some customer service aspect and your client suggests that you just saved his life, or at least his job . . . doesn't that sound like a good time to ask for a referral?
- When you deliver a new product
- During a review or check-up process as part of your service

Make a list of all of the instances in which your firm comes into contact with its clients and referral sources and look for natural opportunities to systematically insert some aspect of your referral marketing system.

The Simplest Referral Tactic on the Planet

The easiest way to generate referrals from your base of clients is to make it part of the deal. I stated this at the outset of this chapter, but now I want to give the actual process I use to make this happen.

When you begin a client relationship, simply explain that you offer great service at unheard of prices because each of your clients understands that a part of the deal is to refer three new clients within three months of becoming a client. It doesn't matter what number you use here, just create something that sounds workable.

When you meet with a new client, simply add some variation of this statement to your lead conversion process: "We know that you will be so thrilled with (our promised result) that at the end of ninety days we intend to ask you to help us identify three other people who, like yourself, need this kind of result." This strategy sends such a strong marketing message that almost every client you present this to will agree.

Some businesses use this strategy so effectively that the only way to become a client of their business is by way of a referral. Do you think these businesses can charge a premium for their services?

Jan Myers, a real estate agent in the Dallas/Ft. Worth area, sets up every sale by telling her prospects that her business survives on referrals and, in order to earn those referrals, her firm is going to give them *wow* service. This way when she asks them for referrals to build her business, they are delighted to give them. She is now turning what she heard frequently, "You guys are the greatest!" into new business. They expect her to ask for referrals because she tells them up front she will (www.themyersteam.com).

There is something very powerful about setting expectations for referrals. When they are agreed upon and all aspects of the deal are met, people don't have a problem living up to the commitment. It is much harder to go back after you have established a relationship with a client, based on a certain set of expectations, and ask for referrals.

The Value-Added Referral Machine

Want a powerful way to add value to your product or service or gain some new customers in a real hurry? Pump up the value. Go out and find businesses that serve your very same target market, and get them to agree to give you some sort of free product or service that either compliments what you sell or, at the very least, is of interest to your target market. It can even be a trial version of a product.

Let's say you are a graphic designer. Do you think you could generate some new clients if you advertised five hundred free business cards with each new logo design? Trust me, there are quality print shops out there that would love to partner with you on this. Five hundred business cards cost them about $15 to print. A savvy print shop owner will understand that is a fair price to pay to acquire a new client.

Gain New Clients

So put the shoe on the other foot. Go out and offer to provide a service to businesses that serve your market and prepare to be introduced to some new business immediately. Let's say you are a marketing consultant. Go to some local small business accounting firms and offer to complete a small business marketing audit for each of their new small business clients for free. It's a pretty compelling offer.

If you got really aggressive about this, imagine how much value you could build around your products or services. This tactic alone could make you the obvious choice when a prospect goes out shopping.

A Blog Network for Referrals

One of my favorite referral marketing strategies involves forming a network of businesses that can help your clients and formally finding ways to refer those providers when your client needs them. So the electrician has a handy list that includes a plumber, heating contractor, roofer, landscaper, and anything else his clients need. Then, since they already trust him, they trust whomever he refers.

Now let's add blogging to the mix. What if you were an accountant and you started a "Small Business Survival" blog and invited your most trusted advisors to author blog posts on ideas that pertained to their expertise. You would cover taxes and accounting, and you would invite a marketing pro, lawyer, financial planner, computer technician, and executive coach to add content with you. Your target market gets the benefit of great content, and you and your referral network become the preferred small business resource. Oh, and I'll bet you can get the hometown business paper to write a story on this unique marketing approach.

Most of the blogging software allows for multiple authors. The Professional version or TypePad does this quite well and still allows you to maintain control of the blog.

Co-brand Your Way to Referrals

Want to break into a new market? One of the greatest ways to do so is to find a business that is already a player in the market and create a tool that will help them gain more business or enhance their value with their existing clients. Then, offer it to them to distribute with you.

Example: A label manufacturer that sells to the food industry for bottle labels creates a guide for labeling on plastic and packs every money and time-saving tip they have into it. Then they take that guide to all of the plastic molders and offer it to their sales force to give to—you guessed it—companies that buy bottles and containers that need labels.

Here's another example. An accountant offers a seminar on disc that outlines the important tax code implications of a certain type of estate planning technique and offers to co-brand the CD with prominent estate attorneys in her town. Who do you think will get the attention, the salesperson or the co-brander?

Five Core Referral Offers

Your referral marketing effort may benefit from specific offers and promotions that take advantage of some creative ways to generate referrals. Below I have outlined several of the classic referral offers. Think of ways to integrate one or all of these into your referral marketing.

Many times it is wise to have your "expectation strategy" in place for new customers but install one of the following to get the interest and participation of your past clients or strategic partners. You can also rotate your referral offers and promote one or more to find the ones that work the most effectively.

1. *Offer special pricing.* If you are looking for referrals from your existing clients, you can develop a special price for those clients who refer a set amount of new business. Then, when a new client asks what the price of a product or service is, you can respond, "Do you want the full price or the special referral price?" This encourages repeat business and can provide a strong incentive to refer on the spot.

2. *Will work for referrals.* If you can target a referral source that has influence with your target market, you can offer him or her a trial service or product in exchange for an endorsement of your products or services, a testimonial, or a place in the next association speaker panel.

   Seek out the leaders in trade groups and organizations that you would like to target and offer to perform a service or let them try your product free of charge. Get them to agree that if they like your product or service as much as you know they will, they will send a letter to the membership of the organization promoting your offer. Then write the letter for them.

3. *Help a worthy cause.* Donate a percentage of business acquired by way of referral to a nonprofit agency. By offering to help a worthy cause, you can increase referrals while improving your community.

   There are many variations on this referral strategy. You can make donations to a designated charity in your referral source's name. You can allow your referral sources to designate a charity of their choice. If you have a product or service the nonprofit agency uses or buys, you can donate that.

   One of the hidden powers behind this strategy is that the nonprofit agencies can become strong referral partners. If they benefit from referring clients, then they may be highly motivated to provide referrals. In many cases, nonprofit agencies have loyal donors, board members, community activists, and volunteers who would be happy to do business with a firm that was providing funding for the nonprofit agency through a referral marketing program.

4. *Give away gift certificates.* Although the use of gift certificates isn't a true referral marketing strategy, it can be great way to generate referrals. If you have a product or service that lends itself to this, you can provide your clients or referral sources gift certificates to use as a referral tool. The idea is that your clients would give the certificates to people they feel would enjoy receiving them. In most cases, these recipients would be new clients willing to try your service by using the certificate.

   A consultant might give certificates for a one-hour evaluation assessment. The value of the assessment, if purchased, might be $150. It is important that the certificate communicate this value. Make sure that what you are giving has a highly perceived value. A plumber could give free service call certificates at each stop and ask the client to hand them out to neighbors.

5. *One hundred percent refund for referrals.* This is one of my personal favorites because not only is it a terribly powerful referral strategy, it presents such a strong offer that it can become a core point of differentiation. In other words, the sales message is so strong, you become known for it.

In this strategy you simply show your clients how they can receive a 100 percent refund on a specific purchase by simply referring five other people who become clients or make a similar purchase. (Again, you work out the numbers that apply to your business.)

The power behind this is three-fold.

First, it helps you land clients because people think, *What the heck, I can get all my money back*, and because it becomes a game for them. Structure your offer in such a way that they get a 20 percent refund (up to 100 percent) every time they refer someone. That way they can keep score. It usually makes sense to put a time limit on the offer as well.

Another very important aspect of this particular strategy is that it has a viral component to it. Anyone who can earn a 100 percent refund will talk about it.

Finally, everyone that comes to your practice by way of this method will already understand the rules of the game and may very well be ready to play the day they become a client. So that's 5 x 5 x 5 x 5 and so on. You do the math!

Reread that last paragraph because it is true of just about any referral marketing strategy you create. That's one of the reasons referral marketing is so powerful.

A Referral by a Different Name

Hopefully, by this point you are beginning to realize just how powerful a referral system can be. When generating referrals becomes a mind-set for you, you will begin to look at almost any other marketing strategy that you may have employed in the past as a way to generate referrals.

There are many ways you can form partnerships with your clients and referral sources that will help all parties generate lots of referrals. The following strategies can be initiated in ways that are mutually beneficial.

Distribute Your Marketing Materials

Create partnerships with firms who serve your target market. Ask these firms to distribute information about your firm or products at their store, in their invoices, or on their Web site. For instance, when electrical contractors go out on a call, they hand clients a coupon for $10 off their next plumbing repair call. The plumbing contractors they have referred do the same in reverse when they make calls.

Alan Schmidt, a retail shop owner in Boonton, New Jersey, created a "coupon special" co-op with local retail businesses by contacting fellow retail and service businesses about working together to promote their respective concerns. Each participant contributes their best loss-leader coupon specially designed to entice customers to either make a purchase or claim a free "no strings" gift just for walking in their store. Customers must fill out a coupon with their name, address, and e-mail to qualify for the special offer. This also creates the mailing list for future marketing.

Each coupon is coded so the origin of sale is known and an agreed upon finder's fee is paid to the originator. This offers an incentive for merchants to pass out their colleagues' coupons.

Send an Endorsement

Asking your referral sources to send letters of endorsement to their clients or network is another way to generate highly qualified leads and referrals.

Imagine striking a deal with another business that has more than ten thousand contacts or clients in a database. This business knows that their client list could really use your product or service, and so they agree to send out a letter to their list in return for a percentage of all sales produced from the mailing. This type of endorsement or joint venture strategy can produce one of the quickest increases in new business possible from any form of marketing.

Even if you have to offer a significant portion of the revenue generated from this offer, you will benefit from the long-term possibilities with these new clients. (Remember, you are going to sell them more products and services.) This type of referral can also substantially increase your credibility with a market. If well-connected leaders in a certain industry are willing to publicly refer you, then you can bet that others in your industry will see this as a sign that they should get to know you as well.

Give and You Shall Receive

As with so many things in life, the best way to get what you want is to give it. This proves true for referrals as well. Get in the habit of referring others, and you will start a cycle that inevitably returns. Creating your own network of vendors and professionals that can help your clients is a great way to make yourself more valuable to your clients as well.

One of the best ways to start a potential strategic partnership with another business is to first become a client of that business. Buy their product or service, send them a testimonial, and then contact the owner of the business. It's amazing how this little investment on your part will pay off when seeking high-quality partnerships.

Ways to Generate Referrals Without Asking

In some cases, businesses can generate a great deal of their referrals without ever directly asking their clients for them. Many businesses, such as home or office service businesses, send their technicians to do their work. In these cases, it can be difficult to receive direct referrals from clients, but smart business owners can tap into what I call *implied referrals*.

An implied referral involves letting your potential clients know that someone they know is a client of yours or is using your service to fix a problem they are experiencing. For example, an electrical contractor goes out to make a service call in a neighborhood and hangs a tag on the doorknob of ten to twelve neighboring homes. There's nothing too exciting about that, but the powerful twist is that the technician adds on the tag, "I was doing work for the Johnsons' at 822, and they wanted you to have a $10 coupon good for your next electrical service need."

Here's another example. Bowers Technology, a computer and network repair firm, goes into an office building for a service call and leaves a note at every business on the floor. Again, they reference the company they are currently doing work for and leave a card in the name of that business.

This tactic is powerful because it is personalized. Even though your client has not actually made a traditional referral, the implication that someone else in the building or neighborhood used your service lends credibility to your marketing effort. It should go without saying that the homeowner or business that you are already doing work for had better be happy with your work.

You can print many types of door hangers and cards to use in your implied referral efforts, but I can't stress enough the importance of taking the time to personalize them with the name of a client or project. Without this step, you are simply distributing advertising materials.

Pardon Our Dust

One of my favorite examples of this tactic comes from a remodeling contractor. When she starts a new job, she sends a personal "pardon our dust" letter to the owners of the homes surrounding her client's. The letter introduces her company and urges the homeowners to call any time day or night if there is a problem with noise or trash or anything. She does occasionally receive a complaint, which she immediately takes care of. But more than anything else, she receives appreciation from her clients, as well as the neighbors. And she gets a lot of referral business from one simple letter.

You can do a series of letters keeping the homeowners up to speed on the progress or showing a photo of the completed work.

Networking

Networking events are not just ways to meet new potential clients; they are ideally suited to expanding your network of resources, as well as referral sources. Many people attend networking events to pass out business cards and introduce themselves to potential new clients. Take advantage of this fact and invite other attendees to tell you what they do. Make note of how these folks might be of service to your clients. Remember the golden referral rule . . . you will receive more referrals if you give more referrals. When you view and use networking events in this manner, you will find that they are much more productive. Instead of being the salesperson, you become the buyer, and people will flock to find out who you are.

I might add that almost every major city has one or more chapters of a group called Business Network International (www.BNI.com). This is a group of business owners and marketers formed for the primary purpose of building powerful referral networks. Each group limits membership to one person per industry to avoid competitive situations. While every chapter is independently run, they get networking for referrals.

Network with the Rich and Famous

One of the quickest ways to get exposure, promote a book, gain an introduction, find a mentor, generate traffic, or launch a product is to gain the endorsement of someone who already has all of those things.

Here's an often-forgotten tip. Famous authors or other celebrities in your industry started out as people. Okay, some are still people, and that's the point. Approach them as such and you may find that your project or organization can gain some very favorable support.

- If you read a book that you loved, write the author and tell them so. (Almost all authors have blogs these days too.)
- If you liked a product, write someone in the organization and offer your testimonial.
- If you find a particularly well-written article in a magazine, write the author and comment on the topic.

You can build a very powerful, high-profile network of mentors, contacts, and champions if you approach it in the right fashion. First off, give before you ask. You know, prove that you aren't just some stalker looking for an author's private e-mail address, and you will get much farther. Buy their book, link to their blog, send them an article or resource that pertains to their work. Build a relationship or at least get on the radar screen. Don't just send off an e-mail asking them to endorse your product. (You may not be the first person that day to do so.)

A couple of more tips. Be bold, but be realistic and polite. Before you hit pay dirt, you may have to hear a time or two, "I'm sorry, Mr./Ms. Big can't talk to you right now. Call back when you're somebody important."

One of my favorite responses was from someone I won't name. I asked this author to do an interview on a radio show I hosted at the time. I promised that we could tape the interview whenever it was convenient. The response was simple and to the point: "I'm sorry, I don't think I'll ever be available."

If you have a plan, and you are personal and sincere, you just might catch your celebrity when she is in a good mood and remembers when she was in your shoes. Above all, be creative. Propose something very specific, and try like heck to propose something that will benefit your prospective big fish.

Make up your target list of people you would love to have in your network and devise a plan to make contact. What's the worst that can happen?

Online Referral Networks

In recent years, a new breed of networking community has cropped up that allows online users to network with other business professionals and potentially find resources and generate referrals. At the very least, these networks allow members to meet like-minded professionals. The two biggest business-related social networks are Ryze and LinkedIn. These sites allow you to build a profile of your expertise and then network with other members in an effort to expand your contacts based on the profiles of other members.

Mining Online

John Hollner of Hollner Promotions in Atlanta, Georgia, has discovered that one of the best ways to find potential referral sources and joint venture (JV) partners online is through advanced Internet research techniques provided by search engines and other sites. He uses the "similar pages" link (or related: theURLyouareresearching command) when searching in Google. Once he has identified one customer or JV partner-type through this method, it usually leads him to others.

He also researches sites linked to a prospect joint venture partner or customer by using the "link:" command before the domain name in a Google search (link:www.ducttapemarketing.com). This shows potential directories where similar people can be found. It can also list other people interested in what his JV partner offers.

If he is looking for local contact, he uses his keywords with the area code or zip code (marketing training 64105) to narrow his search down quickly. Including the word *list* or *directory* can also increase results (www.hollnerpromos.com).

Speak and Grow Opportunities

Let's Hold a Workshop

Workshops are a great way to spread your expertise and build trust with a target market, but they are one of the best referral tools around as well. When you can convince a trade group, client, or related business to sponsor a workshop featuring you as the guest expert, you have effectively created an endorsement from the sponsor. When the sponsoring bank or chamber of commerce markets the event, they are essentially stating that you have something worth hearing and that they trust you.

The other very powerful aspect of a workshop is that it allows you to present your specific expertise to an entire group of prospects all at the same time. And you're in charge the presentation. Done correctly, you may come to view this type of marketing tactic as an orchestrated sales call.

You can, of course, put together workshops on your own, but I have found that when you take a "hosted workshop" approach, your marketing by way of speaking will be much more effective and much less expensive. With the Duct Tape Marketing position of workshops as referral vehicles, you move the risk of promoting the workshop to your host group.

You can start your workshop marketing tactic off by contacting businesses and groups that serve your target market and offer to hold a free workshop that will benefit their clients or members. Be prepared to demonstrate why this makes a good topic, but also understand that there are lots of groups that need speakers for lunch and dinner events. You may need to do a few of these events to get better at them and to start making a name for yourself. My advice initially is to take any speaking opportunities that you can as long as they make some sense for your topic.

Every time I have spoken at an event, I have receive several invitations to speak at other events. It's not that I'm the world's greatest speaker; it's that there is a need for speakers who can present good information. Eventually you will want to start analyzing the potential audience for events to make sure that it aligns with your ideal client.

Of course, you must be able to deliver something of value to those in attendance. You can always introduce your firm and what it does, but you must give good, useful information first. Jump back to the free report I spoke about in the chapter on advertising. If you can create a white paper that your target audience finds useful, you can easily turn that topic into one or more mini-workshops.

Here's how it can work: a painting contractor contacts a large general contractor and proposes a seminar to teach architects how to write better painting specifications and standards. The general contractor gets better-educated architects, and the painter is seen as an industry leader.

For each of these events it is a good idea to have some prepared materials for note-taking purposes as well as some very brief information about you and your products and services. Most organizations are happy to let you do a bit of self-promotion at these events as long as you are subtle.

Joe Costantino of Business Marketing Success, Inc., in Abington, Massachusetts, claims that the most effective tactic he has found to build his consulting business is speaking engagements. When he first started his marketing consulting practice, he joined the local chamber of commerce and immediately volunteered on some of the committees. As he became better established, he let it be known that he would provide marketing seminars to other business owners for free.

After each presentation, he provided an offer to each attendee that is difficult to refuse—a free business-building consultation (forty-five minutes' worth) with absolutely no strings attached. Each time he conducted a free presentation, he acquired four or five paying clients within two to three months after his initial presentation (www.businessmarketingsuccess.com).

Win-Win-Win

One of my favorite partnership workshop strategies is to approach two businesses that market to the same target as you and offer to provide them with a seminar that will benefit their clients. What makes this unique is that by including two other businesses (say a bank and an accounting firm) you greatly enhance the value of the proposal. The accounting firm and the bank both get to offer something valuable to their clients, but they also get to meet some potential clients in the process.

The two partners may actually compete to fill the seats for you, and everyone in attendance is a new referral.

Workshop as Marketing Tool Tips

Since most, if not all, of your speaking engagements will be unpaid events, it is important to remain focused on the primary goals of each event—to be seen as an expert, present useful information, and generate highly qualified prospects.

It is absolutely essential that you leave each event with the name and contact information from as many attendees as possible. (This is like capturing leads that visit your Web site.) Most groups will understand that some amount of marketing from you is the price they are paying for a "free" speaker. The best way to turn your speaking events into marketing events is to develop a lead capturing system based on the two-step strategy.

At the end of your talk, offer a valuable information product for anyone that drops their business card in a bowl you have placed in the back of the room. There are many ways to create a compelling offer, as long as you are mindful that most groups are uncomfortable with speakers that make a hard-sell pitch from the podium.

If you have created a PowerPoint presentation for the talk, offer to send the attendees a copy if they provide you with their contact information.

Alan Amezdroz of the Inner Southern BEC (Business Enterprise Centers) located in Morphettville, South Australia, finds it far more effective when he makes a presentation *not* using a PowerPoint slide show. Instead, he uses a magnetic whiteboard.

Using various colors, he has made some large names of what

his company offers, laminated them, and attached a magnetic strip on the back of each. He speaks about each item as he throws them onto the magnetic white board. He finds that is much more effective, visual, and dynamic (www.isbec.com.au).

Most groups will have no problem with your introducing your products and services as a wrap-up to your valuable content. If you have actual information products to sell, you may also be allowed to offer them to interested participants. In fact, some groups find that their participants like to come away from a presentation with a book or CD related to the presentation.

The key to creating a marketing event is to get agreement with your host on exactly what you intend to do. Once your reputation as a speaker with a valuable message spreads, you can begin to negotiate with marketing and publicity tactics in exchange for a fee. Some groups will actually give you a list of registered attendees if you ask.

Lastly, I like to create a one-page testimonial creator document. At the end of your presentation ask participants to complete a very brief survey to help you make your presentations better. You can offer some free information product in exchange for the completed survey. If you word your survey correctly and are presenting good information, you will receive comments that can be used as testimonials in the promotion of future speaking events.

Some Speaking-as-Marketing Considerations

- Find out as much as you can about the potential attendees.
- Tailor your presentation to the audience.
- Prepare a simple one-page, note-taking handout with your contact information.
- Create an information product to offer in exchange for contact information.

- Create a testimonial feedback page.
- Follow up with the participants within one week of the event.

Elements of an Effective Referral Strategy

At this point it should come as no surprise that I am going to suggest that an effective referral marketing strategy employs a systematic approach along with a compelling referral offer. Here are the basic steps in a successful referral marketing system:

Duct Tape Marketing Chapter Resources

Referral Flood - Referral marketing program
www.ducttapemarketing.com/referral.php

BNI - Referral networking organization
www.ducttapemarketing.com/bni.php

Action Steps

1. Create a referral target market(s). You must create a target list of companies and individuals who can be motivated to refer. This can be clients or a network of related businesses.
2. Design a referral education system.
3. Outline your referral lead offer and system.
4. Create a referral conversion strategy.
5. Identify a referral follow-up strategy.

Chapter Twelve

Automate Your Marketing with Technology Tools

One of the surest ways to kick your marketing efforts into high gear is through the use of tools that help automate various marketing and follow-up activities. Few things will benefit your marketing systems approach more than the ability to consistently follow up with prospects. The trick in employing marketing automation tools is to strike the correct balance between person and machine. Where possible, you want a personal touch that's automated. I like to call this approach *mass personalization*.

Effective mass personalization allows you to automatically reach a great deal of prospects without sacrificing the personal touch. People realize that some of your marketing is being done by machines, and to a point they can accept that, but there are some very basic tactics introduced in this chapter to make your use of technology less "techie" feeling.

Embrace the Internet—or Else

Before I get very deep into this chapter, I must make a bit of a stump speech. No matter what industry you are in, you must embrace the Internet or prepare to get run over by your competition. Okay, if you herd sheep in rural Uzbekistan, maybe you can take your time on this one, but everybody else needs to jump on the train now.

The Internet, and perhaps more specifically Web sites, lost a bit of appeal for small business owners when they came to the realization that simply putting a very poorly written and designed Web site online was not going to make the phone jingle with new business. Many small, locally based businesses continued to sit on the sidelines and assume that since they didn't want business from the World Wide Web, they didn't need a Web site. Those days are way behind us.

Web sites have evolved immeasurably in recent years, and so has the Internet. When I use the term *Web site*, I am including the use of blogs, podcasts, and streaming audio and video delivery in that definition. Suffice it to say that no matter your target market, your prospects expect you to have a Web presence. This means not simply a sales brochure but a Web site that educates, offers value, and involves the visitor in some form of interaction. (And no, when I suggest interaction, I don't mean a spinning "whack a mole" game banner at the top of each page.)

Back in chapter 6, I presented what your Web site should convey in order to supplement your marketing efforts. If you do nothing more than build that kind of site, you will have a useful marketing tool. The primary focus of this chapter is to introduce tools and strategies that will allow you to create a site that captures your visitors' imagination and their contact information.

Web sites are very effective lead generation tools as part of an overall integrated system, but you should also think in terms of your Web site as a powerful way to build trust, personalize your Core Message, connect with clients, extend your advertising message, deliver products, build communities of like-minded clients, and carve out your place as an expert in your industry. Think of your Web site as serving much more than one function. Your Web site can become the marketing tool that holds all of your other marketing activities together.

It is my hope that chapter 6 allowed you to better understand the basic content components of an effective Duct Tape Marketing Web site. In what remains of this chapter, I want to focus on ways to help you get much more from your Web site by helping you understand how to incorporate automated, yet personal, marketing tools into your Web strategy.

A Lead Capture System

When a visitor chooses to stop by your Web site, you have a golden opportunity to make a good impression. But once they are gone, they may be gone forever, without you even knowing they had some momentary interest in your products or services.

Every Duct Tape Marketing Web site possesses a system and strategy for capturing some amount of contact information from your Web site visitors. I use the word *strategy* because I know you've visited Web sites that have sign-up forms of one type or another, but people are reluctant to give over any contact information unless they feel the risk (potentially getting spam) warrants the reward. In most cases, this involves the exchange of something of highly perceived value. In previous chapters, I presented the idea of offering a white paper or free evaluation. These are perfect examples of the kinds of things people will exchange for their contact information.

Once you have this information and permission to continue to market to these prospects, you can build trust through a series of contacts. Many times prospects will start their search for a new product or service by surfing on the Internet or collecting data through other means long prior to actually making a purchase. The marketer that captures this hot lead and continues to provide useful, educational information stands the best chance of converting that lead to a sale when the time is right. Create a compelling offer, place a sign-up form in a prevalent place on your site, and start building an e-mail marketing list made up of your Web site visitors.

You don't always need to send prospects and clients to a Web site to capture this type of data either. Think about retail businesses that attract lookers, home services businesses with many homeowner customers, or beauty salons that offer their clients and prospects something in return for their e-mail contact information. People love contests, so you can offer a monthly drawing for a product or service to entice participation.

Once you have a prospect's basic contact information and permission to send updates and newsletters, you have another powerful means of reaching a highly targeted audience with new product announcements, service upgrades, sales, and other promotional messages. Pick your slowest day of the week and offer an e-mail-list-only special to make the phone ring on that day.

Landing Pages

Think back to the Duct Tape Marketing advertising approach of offering valuable free information. You may recall that I suggested that your advertising should only attempt to do one thing at a time. The purpose of your two-step ad is to get a reader to visit or call to receive your free information, right?

If you send your readers to a Web site, you will find that your promotion is even more successful if you create Web pages specifically designed for your ad promotion. Many people in Internet marketing circles call these landing pages. The idea behind a landing page is that a prospect lands there instead of on the home page for your site. When you design a page that is intent only on spelling out your offer for free information, you will find that more people will actually take the important step of completing a form and giving you their information.

If you send people to your home page, they may have trouble finding your specific offer or may become distracted by other content on your site. While this may not seem like a bad thing, if the purpose of your ad is to distribute information and capture a lead, then you don't want to put up roadblocks or confuse. You can always redirect your visitors to any page on your Web site after they complete your sign-up form.

Another benefit of individualized landing pages is that they are very easy to track. If you run ads in several publications, each pointing to a unique landing page, you have a ready built tracking system for each ad. (This assumes that you have access to your Web site statistics, something you should have and that most Web hosts provide.)

Autoresponders

Autoresponders are automated response e-mail generators and are great tools in the right hands. Autoresponders come in all shapes and sizes as either software that you run on your Web host's computer or as Web-based services such as AWeber (www.AWeber.com).

The basic function of an autoresponder service is to automatically allow you to capture the lead data of your Web site sign-ups, manage your list sign-ups and removals, and send messages to your list. Part of the magic of this service is that these messages can be prewritten and loaded so that they, for example, are automatically sent the moment someone requests your free report.

You can use an autoresponder service to create and automatically send as many messages as you like. For instance, if someone downloads your free tips reports, you can program your service to send out additional tips every week or every month for as long as you like. This type of steady contact, generated automatically, allows you to consistently get your message in front of highly qualified prospects and can also be a great way to provide confirmation and basic download instructions when you are promoting a free report or service.

As you write your autoresponder messages, make sure that you keep education, not sales, as your primary goal, particularly early on. Don't bombard your new subscriber with sales copy. By this point in the book, I really shouldn't need to remind you of that point, but just in case.

Another key to running effective autoresponder messages is to work very hard at giving them a personal touch. Most people realize when they request a free marketing tips newsletter that you are not sitting there waiting at your computer to fire off the first issue when they request it, but here is a tactic that can greatly enhance your message impact. When I set up a series of responses, I program the first to send out exactly what they have requested and perform the basic confirmation. Then I write a very personal sounding message that is sent three or four days after someone has responded to my offer that goes something like this:

Hey (name),

I noticed you subscribed the other day to my newsletter, Duct Tape Marketing. Thanks. I really enjoy producing this content and helping small business owners. If you ever have a question or want to comment on something in the newsletter, don't hesitate to contact me.

You can also visit my Weblog where I post topics of interest to small business owners and give you the ability to post your comments to share with other small business owners (http://www.ducttapemarketing.com/weblog.php).

Thanks again,

John Jantsch

About 10 percent of the people who receive this message write to me to tell me how much they appreciate this personal touch. I'm not suggesting that I'm tricking them with this note; it *is* personal. It is what I believe; it's just presented in a fashion that makes it possible that I wrote it specifically to the reader. That's a good thing.

E-zines, E-mail, and Trust

E-mail is still a very powerful form of communication. Other methods are coming on strong but, just like direct mail, e-mail is still very powerful. Use e-mail to help round out your marketing message and send frequent, subscription-type messages. Again, I don't think that any business should rely solely on one form of communication. Think in terms of setting up numerous forms of communication so you can reach the largest number of prospects with the largest number of messages.

Cindy Kraft, a career management coach in Brandon, Florida, developed a weekly coaching tip that she delivers by e-mail. At first, she targeted her existing client base. Now it has grown exponentially via circulation of my faithful readers.

Every Monday morning she provides career-related expertise to her readers. It is usually brief, a couple of paragraphs. It is also designed to give readers something of value, prompt them to share the information she provides, and drive traffic to her blog where there is even more great career and job-search related information (www.career-management-coach.com).

I've already talked about capturing leads on a Web site or at the cash register, but in order to make this tactic the most powerful, I suggest that you create an online newsletter that allows you to routinely send your prospects more information by way of e-mail. A newsletter can be as simple as a communication that points out one or two valuable pieces of information. As long as you produce useful content, you can even use your newsletter to gently promote and introduce your products and services.

A newsletter can be a great way to establish a bond with your readers over a period of time. Service providers in particular can use a newsletter to slowly educate their readers on a specific practice or expertise. Many business owners find an online newsletter or e-zine perfect for promoting changes within a business or industry or even "subscriber only" sales.

Some E-zine Publishing Tips:

1. *Start strong.* Create your best newsletter and archive it as the one that your readers receive as their first issue.

2. *Be consistent.* In order for most small business e-zines to take root, they need to be sent at least monthly.

3. *Be familiar.* It's okay to experiment with content, but your newsletter will benefit from set sections such as a product or book review. You can be creative too. I love music, so I feature an album in every issue of my newsletter. I get lots of good feedback from this section.

4. *Use a strong subject line that compels the reader to open your e-mail and helps them know it is your newsletter.* It's not enough simply to send a newsletter, you've got to get it read too. Make sure that your subject line has an element that the recipient will recognize and an attention grabbing line that will make them want to open it up. Here's an example: "Subject: Unleash a good virus in your marketing."

5. *Focus on content.* It's okay to introduce products and offer special deals, but the bulk of your newsletter should provide valuable content or people will grow tired of receiving it.

6. *Use a table of contents.* This lets readers scan and find the things that interest them without having to read the entire newsletter.

Use Your Autoresponder to Manage Your E-zine

Your autoresponder service is also a powerful e-zine list management and distribution service. With a service such as AWeber, you can invite Web site or store visitors to sign up and then create your newsletter and broadcast it to your current list of subscribers. Good services will also manage reader requests to unsubscribe and allow you to check to make sure that your newsletter does not contain content that might trigger spam filtering.

HTML vs. Text

An HTML newsletter is a newsletter that arrives in your e-mail inbox but looks like a Web page with full graphics. A text e-mail is text only.

Tests prove that HTML e-mail newsletters generate a much higher readership and response because they are just more interesting and offer the ability to use color and images to enhance your message. They are also a bit harder to create and send.

For most businesses I recommend HTML newsletters because I think the trade off is worth it. A tip: when you use your auto responder to send an HTML newsletter, make sure that you also broadcast a text version with some portion of the newsletter content. This way, people who can't receive HTML e-mail will still receive your message, and the spam filters will have something better to use to verify that your e-mail is the good stuff.

Some HTML Newsletter Tips

There are services that specialize in offering HTML e-mail newsletter templates, but I recommend that you create a newsletter that ties to the look and feel of your Web site as much as possible. If you know how to create Web pages, then doing this is a snap. If not, have a Web designer create a template for you and then learn how to update the template with your content for each issue.

Beware of designs that add extras. E-mail distribution is tricky all by itself, so stick to very basic HTML without any extras.

Also important to remember when designing your newsletter or hiring someone to do it are *width* and *image links*. Here are some guidelines:

Width. Keep the width of your newsletter contained in a table and no more than 600 pixels wide. You want to make sure that your e-mail shows up in the e-mail window of the recipient.

Image links. If you use images, and you probably should, make sure that you use absolute links to the images as opposed to relative links. In traditional Web page design, an image link may be something like this: /images/bob.jpg. This is fine when you are getting the image on your server, but when you send out an e-mail, the recipient needs the entire path to be more like this: http://www.yoursite/images/bob.jpg.

One Final Note about HTML Newsletters

HTML is the language of Web pages. So guess what—since you've gone to the trouble to create an HTML newsletter, you have actually created a Web page. It is a very good idea to upload your HTML newsletter to your Web site and create a newsletter archive. This will give you a place to send readers to get a sample of the wonderful content you create, but it will also add to the overall page quantity and quality of your Web site for those search engine spiders.

Systematic Fulfillment

Your Web site can provide an important link between your two-step advertising promotions and your free information products. When prospects view your two-step ads and visit your Web site to sign up for a free report, e-zine, or online course, you can easily program your autoresponder service to automatically redirect your prospects to another Web page where they can immediately download their report.

You can house many forms of information on your Web site and send prospects to specific pages for more information. For example, I have a number of brief audio programs that I can send prospects to based on the information they request from my Web site. I also have a program that I direct potential clients to just before and directly after meeting with them. This type of interactive communication with clients and prospects allows you to present a very powerful point of differentiation in your marketing efforts. It is unlikely that the businesses you are competing with are providing this type of service.

Partner with Your CRM Software

It's essential that you build and track your database of customers and prospects. There is an entire class of software known as customer relationship management software that allows you to store key contact information along with a host of custom data fields that you can design for your specific needs.

The leading small business CRM titles are ACT, Goldmine, and Maximizer. Online versions such as Salesforce.com and Sunrise are also gaining popularity. Like most software, each has its strengths and weaknesses, but all three can serve your needs very well. A core function of this software is that you can use it to keep track of every contact with a client or prospect. In other words, you can assign monthly mailing codes and know who received what offer. In addition, you can track appointments, meetings, phone calls, and tasks back to each contact.

You can import your autoresponder or other leads directly into your CRM program and print envelopes and labels. The makers of these software programs also offer training and customization services that can help you get the most from the software.

Search Engines—The Local Twist

Each of the major search engines has aggressively staked out an approach to local search. *Local search* is a term that defines the way people have grown to search for local businesses. Search terms like "plumber San Diego fast" are commonplace and return specialized, almost directory-like results for local businesses complete with maps and basic business information.

Google, Yahoo, AOL, and MSN each build their directories in different ways, but it is essential that your business be listed in each for your category of business. In time, these results will overtake printed phone directories and eventually show up in mobile phones as your prospects drive around town. The basic directory listings are free as of this writing. Enhanced listings can be purchased with store hours, product and service descriptions, and specialized pages for items such as menus and coupons.

While I would not advocate this option, it is possible to create a Web presence through local search directories without a traditionally built Web site. Each of the major search engines is adding Web hosting, blogs, and e-mail to its small business mix.

At the moment, pay-per-click advertising available from search companies can be purchased with local-only options.

Blogs—A Natural Marketing Integration Tool

A blog is an easily published Web site content creation that publishes entries in chronological order. That much I hope you know by this time, but blogs are also a tremendous small business marketing tool as well. Blogs offer several very compelling attributes:

- They make creating new content easy for anyone.
- They are looked at very positively by search engines.
- They offer instant interaction and conversation with your prospects.
- The content that is produced is automatically distributed to search engines and subscribers.

From my point of view, though, one of the best reasons to have a blog is that it's simply one more very easy, very affordable method to connect with your prospects and integrate all of your marketing messages. Blogs also force you to write and research new content. No matter what business you think you are in, you are in the information business. Blogging creates information that can be used in a variety of ways. Here are some tips on effective blogging:

1. *Create a narrow niche theme for your blog and stick to it.* It's okay to post an occasional random thought, but remember that your blog is serving a business purpose, and the content should strive to serve that purpose.
2. *Give your blog a name.* Help readers connect to the content much like they might to the name of magazine.
3. *Post often.* Sorry, no room to wiggle on this one. Your readers will abandon your blog unless you post almost daily. Search engines love this too.
4. *Participate in the blogosphere.* Read other blogs, and post comments and trackbacks to other blogs. Link to blogs that you think would be relevant to your blog's readers.
5. *Respond to reader comments on your blog.* One of the primary purposes of a blog is to create client conversations.

6. *Every now and then, post something controversial.* Take a stand on something in your blog and invite reader participation.

RSS—Content Distribution, Aggregation, and Filtering

Whether you know it or not, you have probably consumed some amount of content in the past day or two that was delivered via RSS. As I mentioned in an earlier chapter, RSS is just a term used to define any number of ways to automatically distribute updated content. Blogs, for instance, have built-in RSS syndication features that allow blog search engines and subscribers to get new content as soon as the blog owner posts a new entry. Almost every newspaper and magazine offers some form of topic specific RSS feed.

RSS offers small businesses two distinct marketing opportunities. RSS allows small businesses to publish and distribute content from blogs, press releases, news updates, or even project updates in almost real time without editing a host of Web pages. RSS also allows other Web site owners and news services to publish your content and effectively act as a source of traffic to your Web site.

Equally important, RSS is a fabulous listening tool. Each of the major search engines allows you to create tailored search phrases and terms and then subscribe to these searches. With the use of an RSS reader, you can automatically receive updates when someone on the Internet talks about a specific company, industry, person, or organization.

Think of the possible sales implications of this approach.

By subscribing to feeds that deliver information about your competitors, you may be able to discover what a host of blog writers think a competitor's product weaknesses are. This technology makes it very easy to create custom news and search alerts tailored to each of your clients. Imagine if your #1 client went to the University of Texas and loves rare orchids, and you had the daily highlights from the Longhorn campus paper along with blog posts from the top orchid club in South Africa delivered to your desktop everyday. Do you think that might make it a little easier to stay up on things your client cares about?

Two Web Sites May Be Better Than One

I hope that I've convinced every reader that they need a Web site. In fact, the truth might actually be that you really need two.

Businesses that take the Duct Tape Marketing educational approach may find that they can achieve even greater results when they create one Web site that is specific to their business, product, service, name, etc. and another site that functions purely as an educational site specific to the benefits of their service or product. So JoesBaitShop.com tells all about the various lures and tackle you recommend, even more about the charter trips, and eventually how to make a purchase. CatchFishToday.com (your other site), however, is full of informative articles, how-to tips, and resources for avid fisherpersons.

Of course this site also has plenty (but not too many) of links back to JoesBaitShop.com. This second site may actually be a great place to get content contributed by your network and strategic partners. This approach really allows you to take a leadership role in a specific niche.

An attorney who specializes in construction work may find that he can set up a site that becomes a portal for the construction industry in his community and allows accounting, insurance, and banking partners to add to the overall value of the site.

People don't go online searching for companies; they go online looking for solutions, information, answers to life's persistent questions . . . you know, like what's the best hat to wear cod fishing? Your second Web site gives them the answer and sends them to your first site to go shopping. It really doesn't matter what business you are in. An investment banking firm can benefit from the same strategy.

The major search engines want to index high-quality information. A site that appears to be educational in nature will usually score higher than a site that presents the services of a firm. In addition, search engines pay a great deal of attention to and reward the fact that other Web sites link back to a site. A high-quality "how to" site about a topic is more likely to draw plenty of related links from other Web sites than a company Web site. This will help drive traffic to your company site.

An E-commerce Primer

Many small business owners, particularly those who embrace the Duct Tape Marketing approach of offering information products via a Web site, will find the need to accept credit card payments for products and services offered on their Web site.

When I set up my first e-commerce Web site, I found the information surrounding online credit card purchases to be more confusing than any other aspect of marketing on the Internet. The reason, as it turns out, is that the various organizations offering to advise you on how to set up online payment systems have conflicting interests and, in some cases, no idea how the systems work together.

The other potentially confusing aspect of online payments is that the entire system involves a number of service suppliers, each providing one element of the entire chain. The real trick is getting them all working together. So let me outline the parts and then give you a couple of suggestions for how you might approach an e-commerce system for your business. (There are dozens of ways to get the same thing done!)

Internet Merchant Account

In order to take online payments, when you don't physically swipe a credit card, you need an Internet merchant account. This account can be issued by your bank or by a host of companies that offer merchant accounts. It's important to note that if you already have a merchant account for your store or business, you will need to get an Internet account as they are different. This account will include a set-up fee and some percent-per-transaction fee.

Payment Processor

To actually get the money from a credit card–holding customer and into your bank account, you need a payment processor. This is usually not the same company as the one that provided the merchant account. There are only a handful of processors, and your bank or other merchant account provider will partner with a processor such as First Merchant Solutions.

Most banks only provide merchant accounts for Visa and MasterCard. It is a very good idea to offer American Express and Discover card payment options. In order to do this, you need to contact American Express and Discover and activate accounts. Once you have this information, you can provide it to your merchant account provider's payment processor to process all four cards in the same account.

Secure Payment Gateway

Since Internet traffic is susceptible to eavesdropping, you will need a secure payment gateway that allows your customers' credit card data to be secure as they place orders. This is yet another service provider that specializes in secure transactions and takes the secure data and passes it through a secure gateway to your payment processor. This is available from Authorize.net for a monthly service fee.

If you are selling goods that are available to download immediately, you will also need what is known as real-time processing from your secure processor. This is simply a connection that gets a credit card transaction approved or declined in real time as a customer places an order. There is an additional charge for this service.

Virtual Terminal

A virtual terminal is an add-on service that comes with your Internet merchant account. This allows you to take credit card orders by phone or in person and then go to a secure Internet-based site and process the orders into your account.

Shopping Cart

Shopping carts come in software and hosted-service versions and allow your customers to shop for multiple items and then pass the order to your payment system by way of checkout. This service is very important if you have multiple products available on your Web site. There are some very stable, fully functioning shopping carts that are free or very low cost.

Third-Party Processing

There is an alternative solution to the entire puzzle known as a third-party processor. In this approach, the third party provider may offer all of the processing and no merchant account is required. The drawback to this approach is that you generally pay a higher overall fee per transaction and have limited ability to customize your customer's check out experience to match your Web site. PayPal is the largest provider of this approach and is an acceptable option.

A Few Words of Advice

Each piece of the e-commerce puzzle comes with a fee, either as a monthly set price or on a per transaction basis. Make sure that you understand what the fees are. Online merchant account providers are notorious for charging very high application and set-up fees. Start with your bank, but shop this aspect around. Most small business owners should be able to set up a fully functioning, real-time processed site with a shopping cart for less than $150 per month (not including per transaction fees).

Make sure that you find out which parts work well with each other. In other words, when you are looking for a shopping cart or payment processor, make sure that they integrate with your real-time payment gateway and vice versa. If you stick with the big names in each category, you shouldn't have any problems.

Duct Tape Marketing Chapter Resources

AWeber Communications - Autoresponder service
www.ducttapemarketing.com/aweber.php

Basecamp - Online project and collaboration tool
www.ducttapemarketing.com/basecamp.php

Action Steps

1. Determine your Internet lead capture strategy.
2. Outline your plan to start an online newsletter.
3. Research the possibility of adding a blog to your online marketing activities.

Chapter Thirteen

Turn Prospects into Clients and Clients into Partners with an Advanced Education System

In this chapter, I'm moving the Duct Tape Marketing System away from lead generation, the basic work of generating contacts and referrals, and toward the ultimate goal—lead conversion or sales.

Be forewarned, however, that my approach to sales is much different than anything you might read about in one of the dozens of books that focus on teaching you the tricks of the sales trade. If you've jumped to this chapter in hopes of finding some killer closing techniques, you're bound to be disappointed. I refer to this portion of the system as lead conversion for a reason. If you've done everything I've outlined to this point to generate your leads, then selling them is unnecessary—they're already sold. The only job left is to complete their education and get agreement on the terms of their purchase or working expectations.

Effective Marketing Eliminates the Need for Selling

Confusion on this issue will always exist. That's why so many companies have marketing departments and sales departments.

The only reason you need both is because the marketing department is doing such a lousy job differentiating the business and products, the sales department has to hit the streets and do the educating for them. That's why selling can be such a tough job.

With the Duct Tape Marketing System in place, the focus moves away from selling and toward educating prospects that have already expressed an interest in your business and, more importantly, your unique approach.

But, just as I have presented a set of systematic steps to apply to every aspect of your marketing to this point, I want to start the explanation of the lead conversion process with that same key point. This is a system; it's not a technique.

What Happens When the Phone Actually Rings? A System That Works

So you've managed to make the phone ring. It's a hot prospect on the other end—now what? It's amazing how few small business owners consider this question.

There's no question that certain people are more naturally suited to the role of lead conversion than others. But we're not talking about certain people, we're talking about you and your business. What I want to introduce in this chapter is a system that will allow almost anyone to succeed, even with average lead-conversion skills.

Maybe you're a gifted presenter, but does that mean that everyone in your organization is? What if you could take the most successful salesperson in your organization and successfully duplicate her?

The Duct Tape Marketing lead conversion system relies on three distinct components:

1. Discovery

In discovery, the central goal is to discover if a prospect actually fits your ideal target market. If you've done a good job in your marketing up to this point, you will usually attract qualified prospects. Your lead conversion system should help you quickly make this assessment on an individual basis and continue to deliver the expectations you have set with initial lead generation activity.

2. Presentation

Whether across the desk or over the phone, most businesses do indeed need to present an offer of a product or service to the eventual buyer. The Duct Tape Marketing tool of choice for this step is something I call an Internal Seminar. The Internal Seminar is a quasi-scripted presentation made as part of your initial client meetings.

3. Transaction

The final leg of the lead conversion system is a planned "first purchase" transaction process. In other words, a thought out and consistently executed way to take the order, deliver the goods, or execute an agreement. Put a little flair into this sometimes-awkward step in the client relationship building process, and you are well on your way to order number two and three.

A Selling Pattern Interrupt

When prospective clients call Schloegel Design Remodel, a remodeling company in Kansas City, they experience a process that's a little different than the norm. Most homeowners call a remodeling contractor and ask them to come by the house and discuss their project. Prospects at Schloegel are instead invited to come to Schloegel's offices for the first meeting.

During this meeting they are introduced to the practices that make this firm different, shown an array of stunning projects completed by the firm, and introduced to some past clients by way of video testimonials.

They meet the staff and are introduced to the design remodel process step-by-step. They cover the good and the bad and set the expectations for a successful project.

All of this systematic presenting is done in advance of finding out the specific details of the homeowner's project. This unique approach helps this firm stand out from its competition and creates far better working relationships with people who eventually become clients.

On to the Core Steps: Discovery, Presentation, Transaction

Discovery—Have a Plan

The discovery phase is initiated when prospects call or e-mail you requesting an appointment or asking if you could help them in some manner. It is important that you have a systematic way to handle these requests.

If you call prospects back and engage in an unstructured question-and-answer session, you are likely to lose them to some specific point before they fully grasp what it is that you have to offer. I suggest that you pose a few simple questions in your first contact that will allow you to get a feel for how ready they are to understand the need for your products or services. I like to ask prospects what led them to call me or what's going on in their business that needs fixing. (I always ask for their Web site address, too.)

It's important to cut this first contact off at this point. Resist the urge to tell them all of the great things you can do for them.

Often a call like this will come in out of the blue, and you don't want to wing it. This is a system we are working here.

Another value of this practice is that it projects a professional, selective, and thoughtful approach to your client selection process. I don't mean that you are to play games. But you should be thoughtful and selective about whom you work with. Life's too short to do otherwise. Your measured process will make your business more attractive in the eyes of your prospect.

Next, I immediately reveal my marketing process to help both of us determine if we should build a working relationship. The mere fact that you have a structured approach sends a very good marketing message. Again, in my instance I can usually suggest either a meeting or the need to exchange additional materials based on the answers they give to my first few questions.

Presentation—The Internal Seminar

The Internal Seminar is what some people might define as a sales call; the difference is one of control. There are lots of sales books, courses, and trainers that will tell you to probe for pain, ask leading questions, and listen for opportunities to propose solutions.

My belief is that if you have properly presented your solution and value through your marketing, you are there to reaffirm that your prospect fully understands what you have to offer. I think that is best done through an almost scripted presentation or seminar presented internally to one prospect at a time. The reason this approach works so well is that it allows you to keep control of the information that is presented.

I'm not suggesting that you simply show up and ram your message down the prospect's throat, but I am saying that you should have a systematic process to make your primary points. What I have found is that when you do this, you more accurately communicate the key messages you need to put together to attract the kind of client you know you can best serve.

Many salespeople fall into the trap of simply responding to questions from prospects and attempting to "sell" them by figuring out what their hot buttons are and pushing them. The problem with this approach is that it often leads to clients who don't really fit what you have to offer.

When you take control of the meeting and present your core points in a structured way, you will either connect or you won't, but when you do, it will be the right connection. The structure of your Internal Seminar can allow for plenty of interaction, but like a well-crafted seminar, you are the presenter.

You are already familiar with a great deal of the content needed for your Internal Seminar presentation from the marketing kit chapter. The creation of your Internal Seminar consists of weaving the key elements into a concise message that includes:

- The problem
- Your solution
- Your core difference
- Your story
- A real client example
- How you work
- The expected results

I have a presentation that I first used in free workshops called "The Seven Deadly Sins of Small Business Marketing." When I altered this presentation only slightly and began to use it as the basis of my lead conversion system, my sales calls became contract-signing (order-taking) events. Another benefit of this approach was that because I presented a very structured amount of information, my appointments were cut in half. When you take this approach, you can get very good at making the exact points you need to make.

It may take some time to get good at your Internal Seminar, and yes, you can't deliver it in exactly the same fashion as you might to a room full of workshop attendees, but it's pretty close.

The last step is to get some form of agreement on the next steps. This will certainly mean different things to different types of businesses, but you can't leave your meeting with a simple, "I'll get back to you." You must leave with either a sale or a commitment on what needs to come next to move closer to a sale. Then you either move to the transaction phase or continue the education phase.

Transaction

It's funny how often small business owners will spend months chasing new customers, and then once they land them, they have no process in place to make sure they serve their needs and communicate key information.

Once your prospects determine that they want to become clients you should shift your lead conversion into the final transaction phase. I use the term *transaction* rather loosely as I know some businesses may have an actual cash register-type transaction, while others may simply exchange terms of an agreement. Either way, the actual "how" you do that should be simple, clear, and marketing-based. One of the best ways to move smoothly to the transaction phase of lead conversion with a prospect is to be prepared to do so. When you make a lead conversion call, expect to convert the prospect to a client and simply move the meeting to the next phase when the prospect says yes.

Get the New Customer Off to a Great Start

When new clients say yes, you should be prepared to teach them how to get the most from this new relationship or product by putting a new customer kit in their hands. Your new customer kit, much like your marketing kit, allows new clients to fully understand what to expect now that they are clients. That's right, your educational marketing approach doesn't end once you make a sale. Almost every type of business, service- or product-based, should develop "training" documents that communicate key bits of information. Your new customer kit can contain pages that explain:

- What to expect from us next
- How to contact us if you have a question
- How to get the most from your new product/service
- What we need from you to get started
- What we agreed upon today
- How we invoice for our work
- A copy of our invoice

I believe that creating a series of documents like the ones suggested above and having a systematic step that allows you to communicate this information demonstrates a level of professionalism not always displayed by small businesses. Nothing derails a client relationship faster than failing to set and meet initial expectations.

Another very practical aspect of this approach is that it allows you to gather up front the client details that you need to conduct business. Many salespeople (business owners) are so thrilled that a prospect has said yes, they want to run out the door before anyone can change their mind—this is a mistake.

Whether it is in your initial meeting or in a "getting started" meeting, you need to be crystal clear about how you will work, what you need to provide, what you have promised, and what you expect from them as well.

Finally, you must get the money issue addressed very early. I know that you probably agreed on a price for your product or service, but that's where many small business owners leave the discussion. I think this is generally because most people are a little uncomfortable discussing money. Don't make this mistake. At a minimum you should have a discussion as part of your transaction phase that includes:

- How you charge and invoice
- How you expect to be paid
- What you need to do to make sure your bills get paid (Do you need a purchase order number?)
- Who to contact regarding billing issues
- Affirmation about what you will bill

You should confidently include this information as part of your new customer transaction phase. (You can develop a simple worksheet that allows you to gather the information that you or your accounting staff needs and complete this form in your initial kick-off meeting.) Two things will happen when you do. You will have far fewer payment issues, and you will again present a more professional appearance for your business. You will be doing your clients a favor when you have this discussion up front.

Initiating Higher Education

Now that you have qualified your prospect, presented your case, and completed the first transaction smoothly, your job in lead conversion is done, right? Not exactly. Now is the time to start gently moving your client toward the next purchase. How you do this for your particular business will differ, but—and you knew this was coming—the process starts with education.

Make certain that you also continue to educate your clients on how to get the most from your product or service. How many times have you signed up for some service that really sounded great but never got around to figuring out how to use it? Don't let this happen to you. Provide your clients with training after the sale.

Oftentimes your clients will come to you for one simple product or service, but may actually be candidates for an array of offerings. You can begin to teach them all that you can offer right away. You don't need to be pushy, just make sure that you have the educational tools in place—help upgrade their understanding of what else you can do.

Another aspect of this higher education step concerns working with large organizations. Any time you start a project for a large organization you can initiate your education process by gathering information about the key personnel, needs, and projects going in other departments. Keep this large organization contact happy, and they will be a prime source of introductions and referrals throughout the organization.

Ray Evans of Pegasus Capital Management, Inc., in Overland Park, Kansas, calls his education system a process of being systematically "high-touch" with his firm's clients. They do this through defined procedures regarding all communication with clients. These include quarterly face-to-face meetings, weekly or monthly phone calls, monthly e-mail communications, and quarterly letters or postcards. Their goal is to become an important part of their clients' lives. It also lets them introduce their clients to all the associates in the organization. Using different mediums of communication at various intervals gives their clients opportunities to give feedback (www.pegasuskc.com).

A Word about the Invoice

Not all companies send invoices to their clients, but most do. Remember what we learned back in the foundational first section of this book? Anything coming out of your business that touches your customer is performing a marketing function. Treat your invoices as though they are performing marketing, because they are. Design stunning invoices that reflect your other marketing identity materials. Use them to upsell, resell, and communicate important marketing messages. Treat them as a big deal, no matter how small you think they may be. Don't settle for the generic, software template-style invoices just to save time and a few pennies.

Here's my rationale. You know how I mentioned that the whole money issue trips up a lot of small business owners. There are a lot of deeply seated, psychological things swirling around in most people's heads when it comes to money issues. I think that when you make a big deal out of your invoices, you send the message that you care about your client's money, that you are proud to present this invoice, and that you think it's an honor to exchange their money for your goods and services.

> Treat your invoices as though they are performing marketing, because they are. Design stunning invoices that reflect your other marketing identity materials.

I know that may seem like a lot to ask from a piece of paper, but sometimes that's the only tool you have to send the right message. Try it sometime. Print an invoice on a cheap piece of paper with no color and then print one on a very nice quality sheet of paper with your logo and company colors. Now, which one do you want your client to receive? You've set an expectation in all of your other communications, so keep it up.

Surprise and Delight

In addition to your kick-off meeting, I suggest that you add a bonus feature into your initial transaction process. As part of the process, design a step that allows you to give your new clients more than they anticipated. In other words, immediately surprise them with something more than they expected. This surprise can be a bonus gift with a product, another valuable information product, or even a gift certificate of welcome. (This can come at no cost from an eager strategic partner.)

The point of this step is that it gets the relationship off to a great start and helps new clients reaffirm their decision to do business with you. Even though you have convinced your new clients to trust you enough to give you their business, you are essentially still on a trial basis. They know what you have promised, and that's what they bought. Now start overdelivering to make up the gap between promise and result. It's also a nice way to show that you appreciate your new customer. Any time someone gets something they didn't expect, it is memorable. The surprise or bonus you offer doesn't need to be expensive, just thoughtful and useful.

What's Your Blue Light Special?

Remember the Kmart blue light special? It was created in 1965 by a store manager looking to move slow merchandise and quickly became part of the American lexicon.

Years ago I recall tooling around Kmart with my mom, shopping for back-to-school clothes, when all of a sudden an announcer would blurt out those now famous words, "Attention Kmart shoppers, there's a blue light special on aisle . . ."

Every time it happened, women would wheel their carts

around and head for the special blue light price on cookware awaiting them in aisle seven. Even as a ten-year-old, it was obvious the power this marketing surprise possessed.

People love surprises, and they don't get them much anymore. (Even Kmart has dropped the blue light special.) Build surprises into your marketing efforts; literally, make some sort of a surprise part of your client fulfillment system and transact them without warning:

- The first time someone orders from you, throw in something extra.
- When someone refers business to you, send him a cake.
- Partner with other businesses to create and send a gift certificate pack good for other products and services.
- Toss in a T-shirt, send them a book you like, be creative, and you will remind them what a good decision they made hiring you in the first place.

The thing about surprises is they create word of mouth. People will go on and on about getting something extra, something they didn't expect.

Let me state this systematically. Plan this step into your first delivery promise and make it part of your first customer service actions. Client relationships are a lot like bank accounts. You are constantly making deposits and withdrawals. When clients decide to hire you and then pay you for some aspect of work, they have probably not received the full result of the work. This creates some early "overdraft" potential on your part. It's important to look for ways, like bonuses, to make deposits.

The System Recap, Step-by-Step

The steps involved in the Duct Tape Marketing lead conversion process for my business look like this:

Discovery

- Take a call from a prospect and find out a little background.
- Suggest a meeting either by phone or in person.
- Send pre-meeting materials, including a basic questionnaire.

Presentation

- Present an Internal Seminar.
- Determine the next step.
- Send follow-up education materials and the agreement.

Transaction

- Conduct a new customer meeting.
- Add surprise to the equation.
- Initiate follow-up education.

There are situations where I might add a step for a prospect who needs more information or time to do research. You will ultimately need to discover through testing the steps in the process what meets the needs of your individual business. In some instances, your process will require fewer steps, in others more.

Further Thoughts on Lead Conversion

Consistency Builds Trust

Once you build a system that works for you, it is essential that everyone in the organization use the basic steps in the system. Each person can personalize some of the words, but the

Core Message and core steps must be used by all. Few things build trust like consistency of action and message.

The Stated Purpose of Any Contact

Any time you arrange a meeting either on the phone or in person, you should have a set intended purpose and outcome for the meeting that all agree upon. Not only is this a good practice in terms of efficiency, it is another way to make certain that everyone knows the rules and expectations.

Using Presentations

If you use a PowerPoint or other presentation in your Internal Seminar, make sure that the presentation format doesn't become a distraction. If you are meeting with a ten-person executive committee, then a projected presentation might have a place. If you are simply meeting with one person, a laptop presentation may be a bit intimidating.

I suggest that you create a one-page outline or checklist document that you can use with your Internal Seminar presentation. That way your prospects have a sense of where you are headed at all times. If you stay on track, they will generally allow you to make your core points without interruption.

What Objections Usually Mean

There are libraries filled with books about overcoming sales objections, but I can boil almost every sales objection down to two simple things—the prospects weren't really qualified well enough or they don't have enough information. Even a price objection means that they either couldn't afford what you have to offer in the first place (not qualified) or they don't yet understand how valuable what you have to offer is (not enough information).

Your job then is to simply attempt to solve either objection by way of education. An offshoot of many Duct Tape Marketing lead conversion systems is something called a drip system. A drip system is a method that allows you to automatically refilter your prospects into a communication system that continues to drip more information to them over a long period of time—a year or more.

You can put your prospects who aren't ready to become clients (or who can't seem to make a decision) into this education system and stay in touch easily until they are ready to react. Use your CRM software and the constant contact method described in chapter 12 to put this on autopilot.

Make Yourself Smarter

The Internet, as we've already discovered, is a great place to get the word out about your business and automate many of your marketing activities, but it's also a great way to become a much smarter lead conversion player.

The essential building blocks of trust are value, knowledge, and common ground. Your prospects want to know that you offer something of value, understand their business, and can relate to their world before they will relax their antisalesperson guard a bit. In order to break through quickly with a prospect, not in an effort to trick them but in an effort to get your message heard in the right vein, you need to do some homework. Use the vast array of Internet-based research tools to discover everything you can about your prospects, their business, their industry, and their competitors. Your ability to help them understand how you can provide a solution may actually depend on you having a simple understanding of the jargon they are familiar with using. Your ability to connect personally may reside in your knowledge that they are passionate about supporting the arts. It's all there for you; use it for good.

I once proposed a joint venture with a software firm located in France. I did a bit of research on the founders of the firm and discovered that one of founders had grown up in the United States, in my hometown, and attended the same university as I had. Needless to say, that changed our conversation from the outset. It didn't mean I was any smarter, but it enabled both parties to feel more comfortable.

Beyond Satisfied—Your Customer Service Plan

If you want your customers to come back for more and tell the world all about how wonderful you are, you've got to make certain that your actual product, process, service, or result matches what your marketing promised. Again, it's all about meeting and exceeding expectations—and moving your customers way beyond satisfied.

I've already mentioned how important I think it is to create an invoice that has marketing impact. Now let's talk a little about all of the things that happen between agreeing and invoicing.

Analyzing and improving your processes in areas such as status notification, ordering, estimating, scheduling, proposals, delivery, returns, claims, changes, and billing can pay handsome rewards in marketing terms and may allow you to create competitive advantages you didn't know existed.

Where Customer Service Is Bred

Simply put, the key to growing loyal clients is growing loyal employees.

This is not meant to be a book on hiring and management,

but rest assured every member of your staff can and does perform a marketing function. When you hire staff members, I think that it's critical that you understand and communicate this marketing mind-set. In most businesses, people who come to work with a knack for serving and a willingness to learn possess the makings of a great marketing-based employee.

Beyond that, though, it is absolutely essential that you give them the tools they need to be successful. These tools, I believe, fall into two categories: effective marketing and customer systems and the training to operate them; and the technology that makes doing their job easier.

A great deal of this book has dealt with and stressed the need for marketing systems, but suffice it to say that every aspect of your business will run better if you set up systems that allow your staff to effectively complete necessary tasks. (Plus, then they can spend more time on creating innovative marketing strategies.)

Advice on technology solutions for your business could consume the entire contents of another book altogether, but I believe that your business must invest in technologies that support your people and allow them to effortlessly serve clients. I would put a great deal of emphasis on employing technologies that make it easier for your clients to get the information they want and easier for your staff to access and provide information regarding your work with your clients.

I've already mentioned the use of CRM software for lead generation purposes, but the C in CRM stands for customer (Customer Relationship Management). You should use your CRM software to track and file every contact and request with regard to a client or project. This simple step can allow everyone in your organization to answer a client's question about a project on the spot. Powerful yet inexpensive Web-based project and client management systems are being developed every day. These systems allow your clients to have access to and comment on work in progress in real time, from any Internet connection in the world.

Tools aren't always about computers though. Another example of an employee-empowering tool might be the ability to say yes to certain types of customer requests or offer a certain type of free trial service up to a certain value. This type of investment lets your employees know that you trust them and allows them to make snap marketing decisions when they matter to the customer most. Become a student of new technologies, and you will discover a host of ways to give your small business big-business service. But never forget, if you've got happy employees, you will provide good service and your business will grow.

Create Community

Another very powerful way to build client relationships and generate referrals is to bring your prospects and clients together. What I mean is to actually create opportunities for your clients and prospects to meet each other. This suggestion can take many forms, but the key ingredient is that when your clients meet each other they can form a potentially stronger relationship with you.

I think a couple of things are at work here. When you bring a group of your customers together, they can indeed see firsthand that others, very much like them, put their trust in you. In many small businesses, clients can bear many common characteristics, so providing the opportunity to connect with other small business owners, for example, is a powerful way to increase their connection with you.

Here are several ways I have found to use customer community building as a marketing tool.

Peer-to-Peer Lead Conversion

The focus group format presents an interesting marketing opportunity. Most people think *marketing research* when they think *focus group,* but with a nifty little twist on this concept, you can turn it into a sales conversion machine.

This works particularly well if you can focus on one specific industry group. The idea is to find a group that shares the same frustrations and uses the same language to express them.

Put together a teleconference panel aimed at discussing a common industry issue or growing trend. Invite ten participants, but make sure that at least two of the participants are happy clients that turned to you to solve this frustration. Then, once the group is assembled, you sit back and gently moderate only. If any selling goes on during the call, it must come from your clients only. Let the group talk about the good, the bad, and the ugly. Three things will generally occur from such a session:

1. Your current clients usually feel pretty good about the decision they made (that will lead to more referrals).
2. Other callers come away with a very favorable impression of your place in the market—who else is making this kind of educational effort?
3. Several members of the group will call you the next day and invite you to show them how you can help.

There are any number of ways to add a creative twist or two to this approach, but nothing sells like a current user telling a skeptic, in his own words, how great your product or service is.

The Client-Only Event

Let your clients know that you are holding an event exclusively for them. Instead of making it a simple meet-and-greet, sell the event as a roundtable focused on a specific issue of interest. You may even want to line up a speaker to present new information and facilitate the discussion aspect of the meeting.

Customer Loyalty Tools

There are plenty of companies out there that practice things such as special membership pricing, frequent purchase programs, and even cash incentives as ways to keep customers coming back for more. There are cases where these types of tools may indeed bring people back, but they are often price-motivated and will build loyalty in ways that may not be best for your business. After all, price shoppers are only loyal until they find a better deal. I have found that the strongest loyalty-building tool you can apply when working with your existing clients is communication— frequent, results-based communication.

When you set up systematic contact points with your clients as part of your customer relationship management, you get the feedback you need to address new issues and confront any problems that arise.

Again, with the Handwritten Note

Jeanna Pool of CATALYST Creative, Inc., of Denver, Colorado, wants to know if you've ever had a client thank you for thanking them?

Every single time . . . and she means every time she sends out a thank you to her current and past clients, she gets a handful of phone calls from clients thanking her for thanking them. Plus, she has found that about seven times out of ten, they are ready to hire her for another project or two . . . not to mention she finds that she is one of the only small business owners they work with that actually takes the time and effort to show that kind of appreciation (www.catalystcreativeinc.com).

Client Survey

I think that it is a good idea to conduct systematic surveys with your clients. This can come in the form of a phone call after a service is provided, a survey form accompanying a new product, or an annual or semiannual review. Surveys can help you discover when you let a customer down or how you can make your product instructions better. Large organizations frequently employ surveys, but even if your business only has three clients, you should systematically communicate with them at critical junctures in your working relationship to access how they feel the work is going.

Results

Another valuable customer loyalty tool is something I call a Results Review. If you are in a business that provides services over time to your clients, it is vitally important that you measure whether your client is actually receiving the results they expected. Once you do this, it is equally important that you devise a way to communicate how the expected results compare to the actual results.

Far too often your clients will take for granted the work and the results that your firm is providing and can be tempted to listen to competitors offering the latest new thing. It's very important that you keep your clients informed by creating a system that allows you to track and communicate results achieved.

Subscription and Membership Clients

For many businesses subscription, membership, and retainer fee arrangements are a great way to get and keep customers. Dan Janal of PR LEADS in Excelsior, Minnesota, heard the saying, "It is easier to sell to an existing customer than to get a new customer." So he decided to see what parts of his business could be put on a subscription basis, or automatic renewal basis. He knew that every day his clients were making a decision to use his service or stop. When he went to a model that allowed his clients to use his service on a month-by-month basis with no annual fee and no contracts, he found that clients tended to use his service longer and the billing process was much easier, allowing him to focus on selling more subscriptions (www.prleads.com).

Say Thank You to No, Too

This might be a little hard to swallow for some, but it pays long range dividends and is so very easy to do. Have you ever made a pitch for a client or some new project only to get that voice mail or e-mail telling you that they have decided to go with XYZ company, but thanks anyway. Most people hit delete and move on to the next catch.

I have a very simple bit of marketing wisdom that I would like to pass along for those who intend to be in the game for the long-term. Don't hit delete; hit reply, and send one last marketing message. Phone up the client, write a note, make a contact—say, "Thanks for the opportunity, we appreciated getting to know you, and by the way, here is an article that relates to the problem you were telling us about." Then hit delete and move on.

Here's the philosophy behind that strategy. At the moment prospects are telling you sorry, they are never more receptive to a positive marketing reaction from you. Your ability to say thank you to the no is the start of your next pitch to those clients. I guarantee you that they will remember how you reacted, particularly if you demonstrated in the moment when you seemingly had nothing to gain that you had their best interest at heart.

Action Steps

1. Create your New Customer Kit.
2. Script what you will say to the next prospect when the phone rings.
3. Draft your internal seminar presentation.
4. Determine how you will surprise your next client.
5. Get clear on having the money talk with your prospects.

Part III

Getting on a Roll!

(Find Out What Works and Do More of It)

The Power of Positive Expectancy

Before we dive into the last, somewhat tactical, advice of the Duct Tape Marketing System, I want to interject a marketing suggestion that isn't as tangible or as easily explained as many we have covered up to this point—though I know it works. It's something I've heard called the power of positive expectancy.

How often have you expected that something would work and it did? Now flip that around. How often did you just absolutely know that something was going to fail, and—guess what—it did?

I wish I could go beyond this notion of positive thinking and explain in the precise terminology of quantum physics its actual workings, but I'm a results person. If it gets results, I don't always need to know why. Here's how to apply the power of positive expectancy:

- If you expect your clients to be thrilled with your services—they will.
- If you flat out expect your clients to refer business your way—they will.

- If you know a direct marketing piece will make the phone ring—it will.

Okay, I'm not saying that you don't need a good list, killer copy, and effective design, but you've got to believe your marketing will pay off or you won't bring to it the proper energy and enthusiasm required to work through the trial and error phase.

Have you ever desperately tried to sell something that you didn't really believe in? Hard work, isn't it? On the other hand, have you ever found yourself so excited about a product or service that you found people would almost track you down to buy from you?

This notion of expecting and receiving success is widely accepted in self-help, philosophical, and spiritual circles. Business owners sometimes feel the need for cold hard facts and statistics—logical explanations. But think about this for a minute. When was the last time you made a purchase for purely logical reasons? Almost every buying decision ever made was based on emotion and rationalized with logic.

So, what better way to bring emotion into your marketing than to expect marketing miracles everyday? As we move into the final section of the Duct Tape Marketing System, you have to believe you are going to be on a roll! With this belief, the remaining content of this book is designed to help you do two things: (1) commit your newfound marketing knowledge to an action plan that delivers results, and (2) act as a guide for your continuing marketing education. When you do this effectively, you'll be entirely focused on finding out what is working and doing more of it.

To really get on a roll, there are also some basics of planning, budgeting, and calendaring that we'll address in the next chapter.

Chapter Fourteen

Commit to Your Marketing with a Plan, Budget, and Calendar

So much of what you have read prior to this chapter sought to teach you successful marketing strategies to use in building your Duct Tape Marketing System. It is my hope that you have already begun to explore ways to implement what you have read, but before you can move toward the completion of an integrated plan, it is important to set a series of goals that are tied to your marketing plan, activities, and, eventually, budget.

Set Marketing Goals and Communicate Them

Great volumes have been written about the power of goal setting, but little has been written about the notion of goal setting when it comes to marketing.

For some businesses the very act of setting marketing goals will be a giant step in the direction of achieving them. For others, the process will simply validate the need to focus on a vision for the business.

I have found that the ability to achieve any goal is greatly impacted by the goal's power to motivate you to action, so the more powerful the goal, the more likely it is that you will achieve it. Here are ten elements that can make any goal more achievable:

1. You must *really want* to accomplish the goal. If not, then you must find a way to make it so.
2. You must believe that it is possible to accomplish the goal.
3. You must put the goal in writing.
4. You must list in detail all of the benefits of achieving the goal.
5. You must set a deadline for achieving the goal.
6. You must list what stands in your way of achieving the goal.
7. You must list what skill, knowledge, and people you will need to assist you.
8. You must have a plan to accomplish the goal.
9. You must constantly revise your plan.
10. You must make a commitment.

Goals That support the Duct Tape Marketing System: Vision Goals and Tactical Goals

Vision goals encompass your greater vision for the business and for your life. Questions like, "Where do see your business in five years?" are the genesis of vision-oriented goals.

Tactical goals are much more tangible. Factors such as number of new clients, revenue increase, or profit increase all fall into this category of goal setting. Once you come up with your short-term vision and tactical goals, you should find a way to communicate these goals to everyone in your organization.

Goals for Your Vision

I want to warn you that this next section may be some of the most difficult material presented in this book, but take it to heart and it may be the most fruitful. I know, I know, this is a marketing book, and here I am getting ready to ask you what you want to be when you grow up.

If you picked this book up because your business is stuck in a rut, the answers to the questions I'm about to ask may actually be the key to getting you unstuck. So turn off the phone, unhook from e-mail, and write the answers to the statements below on a sheet of paper.

- What will your business need to look like, act like, and be in order for you to achieve your most important goals in life? In one year? Three years? Five years?
- Describe the ideal experience/relationship you want your clients to have with your business.
- Describe a perfect day at work for you.

Okay, now what needs to change for you to realize any of the pictures above? Your vision marketing goals should flow fairly easily from the answers to that question.

Tactical Goals

Unless you are an accountant, the thought of math may not be that appealing to you. This book does not attempt any foray into the inner workings of accounting, but I have found that, like it or not, your marketing success at many levels is tied to basic accounting principles. At the very least your tactical marketing goals should include projections for:

Revenue. For the most part, revenue is sales. Sales are good, and they keep the machine running, but they are not the entire picture. Your revenue plans must address your capacity to actually service the amount of business your marketing plan generates. Some people simply pick a number that is X percent above last year. If you have not done any type of goal setting or marketing to support that goal in the past, that may be your best approach. The primary point is to have a number that you are shooting for.

Profit. A sale without profits is a recipe for disaster. Many businesses fail to understand how to account for the expenses involved in their business and either price their products and services incorrectly or simply fail to make any profit. This is one of those places where employing the services of an accounting professional can be a very helpful thing! Work with your accountant to help you integrate the money aspects of your business into your marketing.

If your accountant doesn't have an understanding of how to help you do this with reports that can give you snapshots of your marketing goals that relate to the accounting aspects of your business, then it's time to find a new accountant.

Your income. If you are the owner of the business or this business is the source of your income, then it stands to reason that you should set marketing goals tied to your income.

A surprising number of business owners never set any goals for the amount of money they intend to make. Without an income target, you are left to take whatever comes along. So, how much money do you want your business to produce in the next year? Three years? Five years? Further, you should set goals that are tied to your actual marketing tactics:

- Number of active suspects
- Free reports distributed
- Prospects generated
- Appointments made
- Prospects converted to clients
- First-time clients
- Web site visitors
- PR mentions
- Referrals
- Business cards handed out

- Workshops presented
- Testimonials received

A Word about Your Time

After you set goals for revenue, profit, and income, you must begin the process of planning to reach those goals. One important step is to decide the best use of your time in the achievement of your marketing goals.

There is a simple formula that can shock you if you have never given it any thought. The formula has to do with the concept of hourly wages. Many employees think of their pay in terms of so much per hour, but business owners and those on salary don't use this thinking. Therefore, they often lose sight of the fact that time is indeed money. Once you set your revenue, profit, and income goals, you should break them down into the smallest possible measurement: the hour. Let's use the accepted 40 hours per week and 52 weeks in a year as our basis for computing your hourly numbers: 40 x 52 = 1,080. So the typical worker has 1,080 hours a year to generate revenue, profit, and income.

The idea behind this calculation is to demonstrate that if you wish to achieve a revenue goal of $250,000 per year, and you are the sole revenue generator for the firm, then you must be responsible for generating approximately $120/hour in revenue every single day, eight hours a day.

Let's say you set your salary goal at $100,000. Then you must generate around $50/hour over and above all expenses related to your product, service, or running the business. The point of this exercise is to give you a sobering frame of reference to draw from when prioritizing how you use your time each day. (Did you do any $5/hour work today?) I would suggest that you take one day and track how you spend every minute. Then go back and assign a dollar amount to the value of how you spent your time. You might be very surprised at how much time you spend doing things that detract from your goals.

What's the most profitable way for you to spend your time? How much time did you spend on marketing today? The biggest benefit of establishing marketing goals that are tied to specific marketing tactics is that it forces you to develop systems and strategies that help you meet the little pieces of the puzzle. If you meet the little pieces (the parts that most businesses don't even think about—like number of referrals), then the big pieces will fall into place almost magically.

Make It a Game—Have Rules and a Way to Win

In an earlier chapter, I introduced the idea of getting your entire team involved in the marketing. This holds particularly true for the marketing goals. One of the best ways to get your team involved in marketing is to set and communicate marketing goals that allow everyone to play. A sale or a referral usually comes about because several people worked together to make it happen.

Once you create your goals, you will find that they take on even more power if you can enlist some of the proven principles of open book management. Open book management is an entire management and accounting philosophy, but one of the principles is to identify a series of critical activities that contributes to a goal and link some amount of compensation to the achievement of these activities.

What marketing activities, if done consistently, would build momentum around your marketing goals? Can you create a bonus pool of money and give points to employees who complete identified activities? You can make the identified activities as big or as small as you like. Not everyone in your organization can actually make a sale, but they likely contribute to a happy customer in some manner. So give them a way to play along. Challenge them to contribute more fully.

Visionpace, a software development company, follows open book management practices and often ties bonus pool points to marketing activities. For example, programmers achieve bonus points for each post they make to the company's blog. A chance at winning in itself is a very motivator for most human beings. The trick is to make winning and contributing to profitable marketing activities one in the same.

Tell the World Where You Are Headed

Small business owners are so busy shoveling coal and doing the work of the business that this glimmer of a long-term vision they have for the business hardly gets any light. If you have some idea of where you want your business to be in a year—in five years, some day—I say, put it out there for the world to see. Let your clients and prospects know your ultimate goal—even if you have no idea how you will achieve it.

I have found that quite often the world will conspire to help you reach your goal, but only if you make it known. One of the most compelling things about being a small business is this notion of clients and networks coming together to help each other be something greater. It's what makes your story so worth hearing.

I'm often guilty of the "ready, shoot, aim" school of business, but when I share where I want to go with Duct Tape Marketing, people start showing up with shovel in hand. So put it out there. Tell them where you want to go.

Create Your Marketing Tracking Gauge

In order to meet your marketing goals, you must aggressively track your marketing progress. I'm not suggesting you become a slave to the numbers—no one really has the time or the need for that—but I do think you should create a wall-sized poster that keeps your critical marketing goals out front for all to see. Your marketing chart, the process that allows you a daily visual of what's important, what's on track, and what's off track, wields a powerful force of focus on your marketing goals.

The Ultimate Measure of Sticky Marketing

In the end, the ultimate measure of the effectiveness of your marketing comes down to creating and keeping clients. I like to create measurements that keep an eye on this ultimate measure.

While tracking your success keeps you focused and validates your progress, it is also a tool that can help you identify problem areas in your system. If, for instance, you are generating lots of leads, but too few of those leads choose to become clients, you may have a problem with your lead conversion process. On the other hand, if you close most of your appointments but can't get in front of enough prospects, you may need to adjust your advertising or lead generation strategies.

There are three simple reports that most businesses can create as simple spreadsheets and use to track marketing success or, as I call it, stickiness: prospect-to-customer ratio, lead-generation reports, and lead-conversion reports.

Prospect-to-customer ratio. The number of new customers you acquire for your business divided by the number of prospects generated by your lead generation system is your prospect-to-customer ratio. For example, if you generate five new customers in a month and forty-seven people entered your lead generation system by downloading your free report or responding to a direct mail letter, your ratio for the month would be five divided by forty-seven, or 10.6 percent. I know this is a fairly simplistic calculation, but the thing I like about a number like this is that it gives you a very simple way to look at the effectiveness of your marketing.

Almost everything you do with regard to marketing your small business will impact this number. Now that you have this number, make it your rallying cry. Make it a goal to improve this number every single month. What this number should be is impossible for me to suggest as it will vary wildly depending upon your business and your industry. The important thing is that you establish a benchmark number and go to work on improving it.

Lead-generation reports. Since the number of leads generated in any given month is a very critical part of your marketing measurement, I suggest that you create a way to view the number of leads you are generating from every source possible. To do this most effectively, of course, you will need to assign some form of tracking code to each mailing, advertisement, or URL you are promoting.

Simply create a chart or spreadsheet with each possible lead source, and tally the leads generated by each. Don't forget to ask every caller how they heard of you as well. A major reason for doing this level of tracking is to gather data on your most effective promotions and mediums so that you can understand where to best allocate your marketing dollars at all times.

You can't improve what you don't measure!

Lead-conversion reports. As you begin to establish your new marketing system, another very valuable tool is some form of tracking smack in the middle of your lead conversion process. Some businesses might relate this to a commonly used sales tool called a call report.

Use your lead conversion reports to track your sales calls, but make certain that you link it back to your lead generation report. It's funny how often one ad or medium can generate a lot of leads, but very few of those leads turn into clients. Another promotion may not generate very many leads, but they are the right leads, and they turn into new customers.

For certain businesses, a call report might just be an overview of what occurred during the lead conversion meeting. This may seem like busywork, but it may also be very helpful in understanding how to improve upon or duplicate a successful lead conversion system.

B-U-D-G-E-T

Wow! We've come this far, and I'm going to mention the big "B" word for the first time. It's not that I don't think a marketing budget is critical—it's essential. It's that I needed you to understand a great deal about the Duct Tape Marketing System before a discussion on marketing budgets would be appropriate.

Most small business owners I have worked with fall into two budget camps: the "budget, what budget?" camp, and the "percent of sales" camp. Both of these camps are a deadly place to be in my opinion. With no budget designated for marketing, you will do one of two things. Either you will not invest in marketing at all or you will waste marketing dollars that are thrown at the idea of the week. (Remember the copycatter's disease?). The "percent of sales" calculation may be a step in the right direction, but it misses the point of marketing too.

Here's the Duct Tape Marketing System philosophy of marketing budgets: when it comes to a small business marketing budget, *you should spend as little as you possibly can in order to achieve your marketing goals.* (See why those goals are so important?) I don't think that's really even a very radical statement, it's just that nobody told you to think about a marketing budget this way. Now here's the rub. You can't take this approach unless you create a marketing plan, measure your results, and follow through on your plan.

Determine the Client Contribution Factor

To determine how to create a "spend as little as you need to" Duct Tape Marketing budget, you've got to do some more simple math. Note that I've said you should spend as little as you need to, but that is not the same as saying, don't spend money on your marketing. I have tied the entire budget process to your goals so they will either influence or constrain your budget, depending upon how aggressive they are and how much money you are willing and able to invest in achieving them.

Before any of that can be determined, though, you need to take a look at something I call your Client Contribution Factor. This is sort of a fancy way of saying, how much is a new client worth to your business? When you get a new client, you should be able to predict how much revenue that new client will produce over the course of two or three years. What this number will do for you is allow you to understand how much money you can afford to invest to acquire a new client. This should be one of the factors you consider when creating a marketing budget.

It's not perfect, but it certainly warrants your attention. If you are a consultant, for example, and you know that each new client is likely to produce $50,000 worth of revenue for your firm, then you can begin to think in terms of how much you can spend to land each new client.

If you sell a $79 product that never needs replacement parts, the amount you can budget to acquire each new client will be significantly lower than the above consultant and certainly less than $79.

The first step is to attempt to determine what the Client

Contribution Factor for your business is. This may not be a very difficult equation for most small businesses. Look at a list of your ideal clients and determine what your average revenue per client over a three-year period is or could be. (Three years is pretty arbitrary, but a good place to start.)

So at this point we jump back to your new revenue and new client goals to start our thinking on a budget number. If you generated new clients in the past year and can track what you spent on marketing as well, you can theoretically determine what your acquisition cost for each new client was.

Let's recap: I've introduced you to a way to set revenue and new client goals, a method to determine what a new client is worth to your business, and a way to calculate your Client Acquisition Cost. In a perfect world, you would simply take your new client goal and multiply it by your acquisition cost and, viola, a marketing budget. This is fraught with problems because it assumes that you have been working your Duct Tape Marketing System all along, which we know can't be true or why would you be holding this book. So we've got to take what we've learned in this chapter and start applying some Duct Tape magic to it.

Create a Budget and Stick to It

The number we are trying to get to with all of this Duct Tape math is a total marketing budget amount. I'm not really trying to give you a proven method for predicting exactly what you should budget for your marketing as I am attempting to teach you what to focus on in order to correctly predict a return on your future marketing expenditures. If you've never done any amount of marketing budgeting, you've got to start somewhere. At best, we can come up with a calculated guess—and then we'll test our guess. Here are the factors we have so far:

1. Your marketing goals (based on your projected goal for new clients)
2. Your cost to acquire a new client (based on your past marketing expenditures)
3. Your marketing budget

If you would like to add one hundred new clients next year, and your past marketing expenditure of $5,000 yielded twelve clients, your marketing budget for this next year is $41,000 (or roughly the same $416 per new client you spent last year).

Don't panic and don't oversimplify what we are doing here. Your cost to acquire a new client will come way down when you use the strategies and tactics outlined in this book, but I'm attempting to teach you a small business budget system that makes sense.

Here's the main concept to grasp: track and aggressively manage your Client Acquisition Cost as a budgeting tool. Again, there is no "should be" cost to acquire a new client because there are too many variables, but when you shine a light on your budget in this manner, your marketing expenditures are held accountable for producing real, measurable results.

Test, Track, and Adjust Your Budget

So let's say that you have determined that your budget for marketing, based on your goals and the formula above, is $40,000. Take this number and spread it out over an entire year of marketing activity. It doesn't mean that you will actually spend $40,000. You are going to make a plan based on it, and then you will simply role out certain aspects of your marketing plan in small, measured tests and adjust your budget according to results. What you will find very quickly in this method is that you can cut your original budget dramatically once your Duct Tape Marketing

System starts producing your goals for leads, clients, and revenue, and your Client Acquisition Cost falls.

As you prepare your original budget, make sure to consider the following key components presented throughout this book:

- Fixed annual expenses
- Consulting fees
- Graphic design costs
- Printing costs
- Web design costs
- Web site related costs

In addition to the fixed foundation type costs associated with the items above, you need to determine the actual promotional expenditures you plan to test primarily as part of your lead generation system. You will need to acquire direct mail and advertising costs for these expenditures as part of your overall marketing plan:

- Promotion-based expenses
- Direct mail costs
- Advertising costs
- Lead conversion costs
- Customer relationship costs

The Calendar

The next and final step in the Duct Tape Marketing System is to take the planned marketing tactics combined with your marketing budget and create a calendar to track your marketing activities and act as a visual marketing project management system.

In many cases you may simply pick out a marketing budget that you feel your current level of business or cash reserves can support, choose a number of marketing activities that you believe will generate an increased level of business, and plan accordingly. That very system has served many a start-up business adequately enough, but your long-term plan should involve a plan based on predictable results.

Map the Marketing Year by Activity

One of the best ways to lead your business down the path of predictable results is to map out an entire year's worth of marketing activity on a wall-sized calendar. This calendar should include all of your foundational marketing work, such as creating or revising your Web site, as well as any planned lead generation tests and promotions.

At first you may feel overwhelmed by the amount of start-up type work involved in creating many of the tools described in this book, but nothing will change until your marketing changes.

One of my favorite books is by Anne Lamott, titled *Bird by Bird*. In the book, Lamott explains that the title came from something her father told her. Facing a deadline for a school report on birds, she felt overwhelmed and asked her father what to do. She explains that his advice was to take it bird by bird. The same holds true for your marketing. You've got to map out a plan and then complete it a step at a time.

Create a Monthly Marketing Theme

Another planning tool I like to employ is to give each month of the year a marketing theme. This allows you to focus on building the tools and systems that you need for that theme. So March becomes the month to build your referral systems and April is the month to build the tools you need to kick your PR program into gear. You don't need to do everything in a week or two. But do something well each month, and the progress you can make in six months may carry you for years.

Make a Daily Appointment Habit

You are in the marketing business. You are the chief marketing officer. You can't do that job by squeezing in some spare time on Friday. Make an appointment and block out the time every day to do some marketing activity. Write an insert for your marketing kit, call three reporters, schedule a meeting with a strategic partners, research a mailing list, and pen five thank you notes. Now that's what I call a good week in the marketing department. It won't happen until you make it a habit. Figure out how to get that time on your schedule and don't cancel the appointment.

The Powerful Marketing Habit of 5s

I started doing this marketing activity years ago, and it never ceases to amaze me how effective this simple strategy is. Each Monday morning, identify five marketing actions and book them like appointments. Then don't go home on Friday until they are done.

Now, these can be foundational type actions, like writing some Web copy or working on a product, but the real power is in lead generation, selling, and generating referrals:

- Write five handwritten notes thanking clients for their past support and business. This act alone will, over time, generate referrals.
- Call five clients who no longer do business with you and make them an offer they can't refuse today! Some clients leave for good reasons. Let them tell you what those reasons were, and you can win them back.

- Call five existing clients and interview them briefly about ways you could serve them better or new services or products they need. Pay attention to what they say. They understand what makes you unique better than you do. They can help you find your Core Message.
- Call five prospects (I don't usually recommend cold calling, but if you must, this is the way to do it!) and simply offer them a free tip sheet, series of checklists, or how-to report that is housed on your Web site. Don't try to sell them anything, don't try to make an appointment, don't try to probe for more information—offer them the free info you know they need, and shut up. Let your report sell them, and follow up with those who go get the information.

What if you did one of these habits everyday? What would that mean to your business?

Action Steps

1. Craft your marketing goals.
2. Determine how you will measure your marketing success.
3. Create a marketing budget.
4. Create a marketing calendar, and hang it in clear view of all.

Epilogue

Bring Your Plans to Life with a Marketing Snapshot

It is critical that you become a life-long student of the game of marketing. The beauty of the Duct Tape Marketing System is that it can evolve and adapt as your business evolves and adapts. So, in a way, this is both the beginning and the end of this book.

If you did nothing more with this book than scratch out a rough outline of the marketing plans for your business based on the steps below, your business will likely benefit many thousand times the price you paid for this book. But I have so much more in mind for your business.

Let's wrap up with a high-level overview of your primary marketing action steps. Think of this as your mini-crash course of action steps to get you started today as you draw up your absolute plan to rule the world.

Step #0. State Your Primary Marketing Goals for the Year. Until you can get very clear about what needs to happen in order for your marketing system to be successful, you many never have the proper motivation to even attempt the steps in the Duct Tape Marketing System. One year from today, what will your business look like? How will it change? How will it grow?

Step #1. Describe Your Ideal Client. Carve out a narrow target market or narrow market segment and find out everything you can about what people in that market segment want to buy and why they want to buy it. Build a company, or at least a marketing strategy, just for this market and make sure that the world hears that you are better at serving that market than any other business ever thought of. Describe a member of the ideal client market as though he or she is sitting across the table from you at this moment.

Step #2. Write Your Core Message Points. Uncover three or four unique benefits that your business or product can provide to your ideal target market, and then make these points of difference your central marketing themes. If need be, change your entire business model to take advantage of an opportunity to serve a narrow market.

Step #3. Develop Educational Marketing Materials. Create a list of the educational marketing materials your ideal client might find helpful in an attempt to understand the value that your firm has to offer. Don't stop at printed materials. Think about all the ways your ideal client might use to do research on a firm like yours.

Step #4. Outline Your Lead Generation Strategy. Create a list of every conceivable way you can reach your target market. Can you reach them by mail, through public relations efforts, or through a network of referral sources? Or, perhaps, some thoughtful combination of all three. Identify at least one lead-generation tactic for advertising, public relations, and referrals.

Step #5. Describe Your Sales/Education Process. Write down the steps you will take when a prospect contacts your business by way of one of your lead generation strategies. Will you send more information, book an appointment, or provide a scripted presentation over the phone? What are steps two and three in the lead conversion system?

Epilogue

At this point what I should really do is suggest that you go back and reread the entire book one more time, but I know that's not how the world works, or at least the world of small business. So, in true Duct Tape Marketing fashion, it's time to act.

I'm going to warn you that you can't wait until you feel the need to get your marketing perfected before you trot it out there. I know I've given you a step-by-step system, but the market isn't always a logical beast. Don't put off testing a marketing tactic because you are not sure you have every element of this system completed. If you were to implement just 10 percent of what is presented in this book, your business would be 300 percent better off. I know that doesn't make much sense from a math point of view, but that's the power of an effective marketing tactic. I have personally witnessed a well-executed, strategic partnership lead to a 200 percent increase in revenue for a small business.

Plan your entire system, go to work on building your entire system, but today, do one thing that moves your business in the direction of becoming an effective marketing business, and then do it again tomorrow. Yes, I know the phone is ringing, the copier is jammed, and the shipment is late. But you're in the most wonderful business there is—the marketing business—so stick with it. Duct Tape Marketing will make sure it sticks with your customers too.

The Art of Creating a Community

by Guy Kawasaki, author of *The Art of the Start*

A duct tape marketer understands the importance of community building. If you've read this far, you already get that.

Here's my take on the art of creating an ultra-loyal community around your business.

1. Create something worth building a community around. This is a repeated theme in my writing: the key to evangelism, sales, demoing, and building a community is a great product. Frankly, if you create a great product, you may not be able to stop a community from forming even if you tried. By contrast, it's hard to build a community around mundane and mediocre stuff no matter how hard you try.

2. Identify and recruit your thunderlizards—immediately! Most companies are stupid: they go for months and then are surprised: "Never heard of them. You mean there are groups of people forming around our products?" If you have a great product, then pro-act: find the thunderlizards and ask them to build a community. (Indeed, if you cannot find self-appointed evangelists for your product, you may not have created a great product.) If it is a great product, however, just the act of asking these customers to help you is so astoundingly flattering that they'll help you.

3. Assign one person the task of building a community. Sure, many employees would like to build a community, but who wakes

up every day with this task at the top of her list of priorities? Another way to look at this is, "Who's going to get fired if she doesn't build a community?" A community needs a champion—an identifiable hero and inspiration—from within the company to carry the flag for the community. Therefore, hire one less MBA and allocate this headcount to a community champion. This is a twofer: one less MBA and one great community.

4. Give people something concrete to chew on. Communities can't just sit around composing love letters to your CEO about how great she is. This means your product has to be "customizable," "extensible," and "malleable." Think about Adobe Photoshop: if it weren't for the company's plug-in architecture, do you think its community would have developed so quickly? However, giving people something to chew on requires killing corporate hubris and admitting that your engineers did not create the perfect product. Nevertheless, the payoff is huge because once you get people chewing on a product, it's hard to wrest it away from them.

5. Create an open system. There are two requirements of an open system: first, a "SDK" (software development kit). This is software-weenie talk for documentation and tools to supplement a product; second, APIs (application programming interfaces). This is more software-weenie talk for an explanation of how to access the various functions of a product, and it's typically part of a good SDK. I'm using software terminology here, but the point is that you need to provide people with the tools and information to tweak your product whether it is Photoshop, an iPod, or a Harley-Davidson. Here's a non-tech example: An open system school would enable parents to teach courses and provide a manual (SDK) for parents to understand how to do so.

6. Welcome criticism. Most companies feel warm and fuzzy toward their communities as long as these communities toe the

line by continuing to say nice things, buying their products, and never complaining. The minute that the community says anything negative, however, companies freak out and pull back their community efforts. This is a dumb thing to do. A company cannot control its community. This is a long-term relationship, so the company shouldn't file for divorce at the first sign of possible infidelity. Indeed, the more a company welcomes—even celebrates—criticism the stronger its bonds to its community.

7. Foster discourse. The definition of "discourse" is a verbal exchange. The key word here is "exchange." Any company that fosters community building should also participate in the exchange of ideas and opinions. At the basic level of community building, your website should provide a forum where customers can engage in discourse with one another as well as with the company's employees. At the bleeding edge of community building, your CEO participates in community events too. This doesn't mean that you let the community run your company, but you should listen to what they have to say.

8. Publicize the existence of the community. If you're going to all the trouble of catalyzing a community, don't hide it under a bushel. Your community should be an integral part of your sales and marketing efforts. Check out, for instance, this part of the Harley-Davidson web site dedicated to the HOG (Harley Owners Group). If you search for "user group" (with quotes) at Apple's site, you get 112 matches. (The same search at Microsoft's site yields 16,925 matches—I'm still pondering what this means!)

Guy Kawasaki
blog.guykawasaki.com

Appendix A:
Further Reading and Resources by Chapter

Introduction: A Solution to *THE* Small Business Problem

The E-Myth Revisited: Why Most Small Businesses Don't Work and What to Do about It (Paperback) by Michael E. Gerber

The Small Business Bible: Everything You Need to Know to Succeed in Your Small Business (Paperback) by Steven D. Strauss

Art of the Start: The Time-Tested, Battle-Hardned Guide for Anyone Starting Anything (Hardcover) by Guy Kawasaki

Chapter One: Identify Your Ideal Client

The 7 Irrefutable Rules of Small Business Growth (Paperback) by Steven S. Little

Blue Ocean Strategy: How to Create Uncontested Market Space and Make the Competition Irrelevant by W. Chan Kim, Renee Mauborgne

Chapter Two: Discover Your Core Marketing Message

Indispensable: How to Become the Company That Your Customers Can't Live Without (Hardcover) by Joe Calloway

The Invisible Touch: The Four Keys to Modern Marketing (Hardcover) by Harry Beckwith

How to Win Friends & Influence People (Mass Market Paperback) by Dale Carnegie

Positioning: The Battle for Your Mind (Paperback) by Al Ries, Jack Trout

Chapter Three: Wake Up the Senses with an Image to Match Your Message

Brain Tattoos: Creating Unique Brands That Stick in Your Customers' Minds (Paperback) by Karen Post

The 22 Immutable Laws of Branding (Paperback) by Al Ries, Laura Ries

Chapter Four: Create Products and Services for Every Stage of Client Development

Customer Loyalty: How to Earn It, How to Keep It, New and Revised Edition (Paperback) by Jill Griffin

Permission Marketing: Turning Strangers into Friends and Friends into Customers (Hardcover) by Seth Godin

Appendix A: Further Reading and Resources by Chapter

Chapter Five: Produce Marketing Materials That Educate

The Copywriter's Handbook: A Step-by-Step Guide to Writing Copy That Sells (Paperback) by Robert W. Bly *Creating Customer Evangelists: How Loyal Customers Become a Volunteer Sales Force* (Hardcover) by Ben McConnell, Jackie Huba

Chapter Six: A Web Site That Works Day and Night

Head First HTML with CSS & XHTML (Head First) (Paperback) by Eric Freeman, Elisabeth Freeman
Don't Make Me Think: A Common Sense Approach to Web Usability (Paperback) by Steve Krug
The Online Copywriter's Handbook: Everything You Need to Know to Write Electronic Copy That Sells (Paperback) by Robert W. Bly
Persuasive Online Copywriting: How to Take Your Words to the Bank (Paperback) by Bryan Eisenberg, Jeffrey Eisenberg, Lisa T. Davis

Chapter Seven: Get Your Entire Team Involved in Marketing

The Experience Economy: Work Is Theatre & Every Business a Stage (Hardcover) by B. Joseph Pine II, James H. Gilmore
Leadership Is an Art (Paperback) by Max Depree

Chapter Eight: Run Advertising That Gets Results

Advertising Secrets of the Written Word: The Ultimate Resource on How to Write Powerful Advertising Copy from One of America's Top Copywriters and Mail Order Entrepreneurs (Hardcover) by Joseph Sugarman
Tested Advertising Methods (Prentice Hall Business Classics) (Paperback) by John Caples, Fred E. Hahn
Winning Results with Google AdWords (Paperback) by Andrew Goodman

Chapter Nine: Direct Mail Is an Ideal Target Medium

2,239 Tested Secrets for Direct Marketing Success: The Pros Tell You Their Time-Proven Secrets (Paperback) by Denny Hatch, Don Jackson
The Ultimate Sales Letter: Boost Your Sales with Powerful Sales Letters, Based on Madison Avenue Techniques (Paperback) by Dan S. Kennedy

Chapter Ten: Earned Media Attention and Expert Status

Get Slightly Famous: Become a Celebrity in Your Field and Attract More Business with Less Effort (Paperback) by Steven Van Yoder

How to Position Yourself as the Obvious Expert: Turbocharge Your Consulting or Coaching Business Now! (Paperback) by Elsom Eldridge, Mark Eldridge

Feeding the Media Beast: An Easy Recipe for Great Publicity (Paperback) by Mark Mathis

Chapter Eleven: Ramp Up a Systematic Referral Machine

Business by Referral: Painless Ways to Generate New Business (Paperback) by Ivan Misner

Never Eat Alone: And Other Secrets to Success, One Relationship at a Time (Hardcover) by Keith Ferrazzi, Tahl Raz

The Anatomy of Buzz: How to Create Word of Mouth Marketing (Paperback) by Emanuel Rosen

Chapter Twelve: Automate Your Marketing with Technology Tools

The Search: How Google and Its Rivals Rewrote the Rules of Business and Transformed Our Culture (Hardcover) by John Battelle

Naked Conversations: How Blogs Are Changing the Way Businesses Talk with Customers (Hardcover) by Robert Scoble, Shel Israel

Search Engine Advertising: Buying Your Way to the Top to Increase Sales (Voices That Matter) (Paperback) by Catherine Seda

Chapter Thirteen: Turn Prospects into Clients and Clients into Partners with an Advanced Education System

How to Become a Rainmaker: The Rules for Getting and Keeping Customers and Clients (Hardcover) by Jeffrey J. Fox

Guerrilla Selling (Guerrilla Marketing) (Paperback) by Orvel Ray Wilson, William K Gallagher

Bag the Elephant: How to Win and Keep Big Customers (Hardcover) by Steve Kaplan

The Little Red Book of Selling: 12.5 Principles of Sales Greatness (Hardcover) by Jeffrey Gitomer

Selling to Big Companies (Paperback) by Jill Konrath

Chapter Fourteen: Commit to Your Marketing with a Plan, Budget, and Calendar

Free Agent Nation: The Future of Working for Yourself (Paperback) by Daniel H. Pink

TurboCoach: A Powerful System for Achieving Breakthrough Career Success (Hardcover) by Brian Tracy, Campbell Fraser

Appendix A: Further Reading and Resources by Chapter

Getting Things Done: The Art of Stress-Free Productivity by: David Allen
Epilogue: Bring Your Plans to Life with a Marketing Snapshot

PyroMarketing: The Four-Step Strategy to Ignite Customer Evangelists and Keep Them for Life (Hardcover) by Greg Stielstra
Steal These Ideas!: Marketing Secrets That Will Make You a Star (Hardcover) by Steve Cone

Afterword: The Art of Creating a Community

Art of the Start: The Time Tested, Battle-Hardened Guide for Anyone Starting Anything (Hardcover) by Guy Kawasaki

Appendix B:
Duct Tape Marketing Small
Business Marketing Resources

Duct Tape Marketing Newsletter
Sign up to receive free, weekly, small business marketing tips, tactics, and resources via e-mail by subscribing to the Duct Tape Marketing online newsletter.
http://www.ducttapemarketing.com/newsletter.htm

Duct Tape Marketing Blog
Visit the frequently updated Duct Tape Marketing Blog and subscribe via RSS or e-mail so that you don't miss a single post.
http://www.ducttapemarketing.com/weblog.php

Duct Tape Marketing Book Tools Web site
Download and utilize a growing collection of marketing tools, worksheets, and forms designed to help you implement the strategies and tactics outlined in each chapter of this book.
http://www.ducttapemarketing.com/book.htm

Duct Tape Marketing Products
Visit our library of small business marketing products, including detailed workbooks and audio programs covering specific areas of small business marketing. Duct Tape Marketing brand merchandise is also available in the product center.
http://www.ducttapemarketing.com/products.htm

Duct Tape Marketing Small Business Coaching
Retain the services of a Duct Tape Marketing Authorized Coach to help you implement the strategies and tactics covered in this book. Engagements are available by phone or onsite. Find a coach near you.
http://www.ducttapemarketing.com/coaching.htm

Duct Tape Marketing Licensing Opportunity
Become a Duct Tape Marketing Authorized Coach. Are you a marketing or business consultant looking for a packaged system and set of tools to help you work with clients and grow your practice? Opportunities to license the Duct Tape Marketing System and brand are available to select marketing professionals.
http://www.ducttapemarketingcoach.com/

Appendix C:
Special Offers

FREE 30 MINUTE
MARKETING COACHING SESSION

After reading *Duct Tape Marketing* you may decide that you want to take action and create your very own marketing system.

You don't have to go it alone. You can engage an authorized *Duct Tape Marketing* coach to work with you to create and implement the systems, strategies and tactics contained in this book.

Duct Tape Marketing readers can request a free 30 minute coaching session from any *Duct Tape Marketing* authorized coach to evaluate your current marketing and get a host of quick tips aimed at getting you on the road to marketing success.

VISIT
www.ducttapemarketingcoach.com/findacoach. php

TO FIND A COACH NEAR YOU.

About the Author

John Jantsch is the owner of Jantsch Communications and creator of the Duct Tape Marketing System. He is a recognized expert in the area of small business marketing. For over twenty years he has coached and consulted small business owners and independent professionals in simple and low-cost methods for growing and promoting their businesses.

Jantsch is an award-winning small business marketing blogger who has developed a special knack for showing small business owners how to harness the Internet as a marketing tool. His blog, Duct Tape Marketing, was recognized by *Forbes* magazine as the best blog on small business and was also chosen in 2004 and 2005 as the best blog on small business marketing by the readers of *Marketing Sherpa*.

He is a frequent contributor and presenter on small business marketing topics, and his expertise is tapped by organizations such as Hewlett Packard and American Express as a small business marketing spokesperson.

He is the author of three complete small business marketing courses: The Ultimate Small Business Marketing System, which is a companion to this book and includes 15 workbooks and 12 audio CDs; Blog Lightning and Referral Flood. Blog Lightning, which is a step-by-step guide that shows readers how to create and promote a blog; and Referral Flood, which is a systematic approach to creating a referral marketing program.